STUDY GUIDE AND WORKING PAPERS CHAPTERS 1–12

COLLEGE ACCOUNTING
Eleventh Edition

Jeffrey Slater
North Shore Community College
Danvers, Massachusetts

Prentice Hall

Boston   Columbus   Indianapolis   New York   San Francisco   Upper Saddle River
Amsterdam   Cape Town   Dubai   London   Madrid   Milan   Munich   Paris
Montreal   Toronto   Delhi   Mexico City   Sao Paulo   Sydney   Hong Kong   Seoul
Singapore   Taipei   Tokyo

VP/Editorial Director: Natalie Anderson
AVP/Executive Editor: Jodi McPherson
Development Editor: Karen Misler
Assistant Editor: Melissa Arlio
Editorial Assistant: Christina Rumbaugh
AVP/Director of Marketing: Kate Valentine
Senior Marketing Manager: Maggie Moylan Leen
Marketing Assistant: Justin Jacob
Senior Managing Editor: Cynthia Zonneveld
Project Manager: Rhonda Aversa

Senior Operations Specialist: Nick Sklitsis
Senior Art Director: Jonathan Boylan
AVP/Director of Product Development: Lisa Strite
Media Editors: Ashley Lulling/Allison Longley
Media Project Manager, Production: John Cassar
Full-Service Project Management: GEX Publishing Services
Composition: GEX Publishing Services
Printer/Binder: Courier/Kendallville
Cover Printer: Lehigh-Phoenix Color/Hagerstown
Text Font: Times Roman 10/12

Copyright © 2010, 2007, 2005, 2002, 1999 Pearson Education, Inc., publishing as Prentice Hall, Upper Saddle River. All rights reserved. Manufactured in the United States of America. This publication is protected by Copyright, and permission should be obtained from the publisher prior to any prohibited reproduction, storage in a retrieval system, or transmission in any form or by any means, electronic, mechanical, photocopying, recording, or likewise. To obtain permission(s) to use material from this work, please submit a written request to Pearson Education, Inc., Permissions Department, One Lake Street, Upper Saddle River, New Jersey 07458.

Many of the designations by manufacturers and seller to distinguish their products are claimed as trademarks. Where those designations appear in this book, and the publisher was aware of a trademark claim, the designations have been printed in initial caps or all caps.

Pearson Prentice Hall™ is a trademark of Pearson Education, Inc.
Pearson® is a registered trademark of Pearson plc
Prentice Hall® is a registered trademark of Pearson Education, Inc.

Pearson Education LTD.
Pearson Education Singapore, Pte. Ltd
Pearson Education, Canada, Ltd
Pearson Education–Japan

Pearson Education Australia PTY, Limited
Pearson Education North Asia Ltd
Pearson Educación de Mexico, S.A. de C.V.
Pearson Education Malaysia, Pte. Ltd

Prentice Hall
is an imprint of

www.pearsonhighered.com

10 9 8 7 6 5 4 3 2
ISBN 10: 0-13-606572-4
ISBN 13: 978-0-13-606572-2

Contents

STUDY GUIDE AND WORKING PAPERS CHAPTERS 1–12

Chapter 1	Introduction to Accounting Concepts and Procedures	SG-1
Chapter 2	Debits and Credits: Analyzing and Recording Business Transactions	SG-24
Chapter 3	Beginning the Accounting Cycle: Journalizing, Posting, and the Trial Balance	SG-50
Chapter 4	The Accounting Cycle Continued: Preparing Worksheets and Financial Statements	SG-97
Chapter 5	The Accounting Cycle Completed: Adjusting, Closing, and the Post-Closing Trial Balance	SG-117
Chapter 6	Banking Procedures and Control of Cash	SG-186
Chapter 7	Payroll Concepts and Procedures—Employee Taxes	SG-214
Chapter 8	The Employer's Tax Responsibilities: Principles and Procedures	SG-233
Chapter 9	Sales and Cash Receipts	SG-258
Chapter 10	Purchases and Cash Payments	SG-298
Appendix 10A	Special Journals	SG-349
Chapter 11	Preparing a Worksheet for a Merchandise Company	SG-378
Chapter 12	Completion of the Accounting Cycle for a Merchandise Company	SG-386

INTRODUCTION TO ACCOUNTING CONCEPTS AND PROCEDURES

SELF-REVIEW QUIZ 1-1

GRACIE RYAN REAL ESTATE

	ASSETS			=	LIABILITIES	+	OWNER'S EQUITY
	Cash	+	Computer Equipment	=	Accounts Payable	+	Gracie Ryan, Capital
TRANSACTION 1	_____		_____		_____		_____
NEW BALANCE	_____		_____	=	_____		_____
TRANSACTION 2	_____		_____		_____		_____
NEW BALANCE	_____		_____	=	_____		_____
TRANSACTION 3	_____		_____		_____		_____
ENDING BALANCE	_____	+	_____	=	_____	+	_____
				=			

Name _____ Class _____ Date _____

SELF-REVIEW QUIZ 1-2

_____
_____
_____

ASSETS					LIABILITIES AND OWNER'S EQUITY				

SELF-REVIEW QUIZ 1-3

B. BING CO.

	ASSETS			=	LIABILITIES	+	OWNER'S EQUITY				
	Cash	+	Accounts Receivable	+	Cleaning Equipment	=	Accounts Payable	+	B. Bing, Capital	−	B. Bing Withd.	+	Revenue	−	Expenses
Beg. Balance	$10,000	+	$2,500	+	$6,500	=	$1,000	+	$11,800	−	$800	+	$9,000	−	$2,000
1.															
Balance															
2.															
Balance															
3.															
Balance															
4.															
Balance															
5.															
Ending Balance		+		+		=		+		−		+		−	

SG-3

Name _____ Class _____ Date _____

SELF-REVIEW QUIZ 1-4

(1)

(2)

SG-4

Name _____ Class _____ Date _____

(3)

ASSETS				LIABILITIES AND OWNER'S EQUITY			

Name _____ Class _____ Date _____

FORMS FOR DEMONSTRATION PROBLEM

(A)

MICHAEL BROWN, ATTORNEY AT LAW

ASSETS = LIABILITIES + OWNER'S EQUITY

	Cash	+	Accounts Receivable	+	Office Equipment	=	Accounts Payable	+	M. Brown, Capital	−	M. Brown, Withd.	+	Legal fees	−	Expenses
1.															
Balance															
2.															
Balance															
3.															
Balance															
4.															
Balance															
5.															
Balance															
6.															
Balance															
7.															
Balance															
8.															
Balance															
9.															
Ending Balance															

DEMONSTRATION PROBLEM (CONTINUED)

B-1

MICHAEL BROWN, ATTORNEY AT LAW
INCOME STATEMENT
FOR MONTH ENDED JUNE 30, 200X

B-2

MICHAEL BROWN, ATTORNEY AT LAW
STATEMENT OF OWNER'S EQUITY
FOR MONTH ENDED JUNE 30, 200X

B-3

MICHAEL BROWN, ATTORNEY AT LAW
BALANCE SHEET
JUNE 30, 200X

ASSETS | LIABILITIES AND OWNER'S EQUITY

Name _____ Class _____ Date _____

CHAPTER 1
FORMS FOR CLASSROOM DEMONSTRATION EXERCISES SET A OR SET B

1. A. _____
   B. _____
   C. _____
   D. _____
   E. _____
   F. _____

2. A. _____
   B. _____
   C. _____

3. A. _____
   B. _____

4. _____
   _____
   _____

5. _____
   _____
   _____
   _____
   _____

6. _____
   _____
   _____
   _____

7. A. _____
   B. _____
   C. _____
   D. _____

8. A. _____
   B. _____
   C. _____
   D. _____
   E. _____
   F. _____
   G. _____
   H. _____

9. A. _____
   B. _____
   C. _____
   D. _____

Name _____ Class _____ Date _____

FORMS FOR EXERCISES

1-1.

A. _____
B. _____
C. _____

1-2.

	ASSETS	=	LIABILITIES	+	OWNER'S EQUITY
A.					
B.					
C.					

1-3.

RANGE CO.
BALANCE SHEET
NOVEMBER 30, 200X

ASSETS			LIABILITIES AND OWNER'S EQUITY		

SG-9

EXERCISES (CONTINUED)

1-4.

Cash	+	Accounts Receivable	+	Computer Equipment	=	Accounts Payable	+	B. Bell Capital	−	B. Bell Withd.	+	Revenue	−	Expenses
ASSETS					= LIABILITIES +			OWNER'S EQUITY						

A.
B.
C.
D.
E.
F.
G.
Ending Balance

Name _____ Class _____ Date _____

EXERCISES (CONCLUDED)

1-5.

(A)

FRENCH REALTY
INCOME STATEMENT
FOR MONTH ENDED JUNE 30, 200X

(B)

FRENCH REALTY
STATEMENT OF OWNER'S EQUITY
FOR MONTH ENDED JUNE 30, 200X

(C)

FRENCH REALTY
BALANCE SHEET
JUNE 30, 200X

ASSETS   LIABILITIES AND OWNER'S EQUITY

SG-11

Name _____ Class _____ Date _____

END OF CHAPTER PROBLEMS

PROBLEM 1A-1 OR PROBLEM 1B-1

MIA'S NAIL SPA

	ASSETS			=	LIABILITIES	+	OWNER'S EQUITY
	Cash	+	Store Equipment	=	Accounts Payable	+	Mia Annabelle, Capital
TRANSACTION A							
NEW BALANCE							
TRANSACTION B							
NEW BALANCE							
TRANSACTION C							
NEW BALANCE							
TRANSACTION D							
ENDING BALANCE							

PROBLEM 1A-2 OR PROBLEM 1B-2

SEE'S INTERNET SERVICE
BALANCE SHEET
SEPTEMBER 30, 200X

ASSETS				LIABILITIES AND OWNER'S EQUITY			

SG-12

Name _____ Class _____ Date _____

PROBLEM 1A-3 OR PROBLEM 1B-3

RICK FOX TYPING SERVICE

	ASSETS			= LIABILITIES +	OWNER'S EQUITY		
Cash	+ Accounts Receivable	+ Office Equipment	=	Accounts Payable	+ R. Fox, Capital	− R. Fox, Withd.	+ Typing Revenue − Expenses

A.
BALANCE
B.
BALANCE
C.
BALANCE
D.
BALANCE
E.
BALANCE
F.
BALANCE
G.
BALANCE
H.
ENDING BALANCE

SG-13

PROBLEM 1A-4 OR PROBLEM 1B-4

(A)

WEST STENCILING SERVICE
INCOME STATEMENT
FOR MONTH ENDED JUNE 30, 200X

(B)

WEST STENCILING SERVICE
STATEMENT OF OWNER'S EQUITY
FOR MONTH ENDED JUNE 30, 200X

PROBLEM 1A-4 OR PROBLEM 1B-4 (CONCLUDED)

(C)

WEST STENCILING SERVICE
BALANCE SHEET
JUNE 30, 200X

ASSETS			LIABILITIES AND OWNER'S EQUITY		

SG-15

Name _____ Class _____ Date _____

PROBLEM 1A-5 OR PROBLEM 1B-5

TOBEY'S CATERING SERVICE

ASSETS = LIABILITIES + OWNER'S EQUITY

(A)

	Cash	+	Accounts Receivable	+	Equipment	=	Accounts Payable	+	J. Tobey, Capital	−	J. Tobey, Withd.	+	Catering Revenue	−	Expenses
10/25															
BALANCE															
10/27															
BALANCE															
10/28															
BALANCE															
10/29															
BALANCE															
11/1															
BALANCE															
11/5															
BALANCE															
11/8															
BALANCE															
11/10															
BALANCE															
11/15															
BALANCE															
11/17															
BALANCE															
11/20															
BALANCE															
11/25															
BALANCE															
11/28															
BALANCE															
11/30															
END. BAL.															

Name _____ Class _____ Date _____

PROBLEM 1A-5 OR PROBLEM 1B-5 (CONTINUED)

(B)

TOBEY'S CATERING SERVICE
BALANCE SHEET
OCTOBER 31, 200X

ASSETS | LIABILITIES AND OWNER'S EQUITY

(C)

TOBEY'S CATERING SERVICE
INCOME STATEMENT
FOR MONTH ENDED NOVEMBER 30, 200X

PROBLEM 1A-5 OR PROBLEM 1B-5 (CONCLUDED)

(D)

TOBEY'S CATERING SERVICE
STATEMENT OF OWNER'S EQUITY
FOR MONTH ENDED NOVEMBER 30, 200X

(E)

TOBEY'S CATERING SERVICE
BALANCE SHEET
NOVEMBER 30, 200X

ASSETS   LIABILITIES AND OWNER'S EQUITY

CHAPTER 1
SUMMARY PRACTICE TEST:
INTRODUCTION TO ACCOUNTING CONCEPTS AND PROCEDURES

Part I Instructions

Fill in the blank(s) to complete the statement.

1. _____ was passed to prevent corporate fraud.
2. _____ – Liabilities = Owner's Equity
3. The owner's current investment or equity in the assets of a business is called _____.
4. A list of assets, liabilities, and owner's equity as of a particular date is reported on a(n) _____ _____.
5. _____ create an outward or potential outward flow of assets.
6. Revenue earned not on account creates an asset entitled _____.
7. _____ record personal expenses that are not related to the business. They are a subdivision of owner's equity.
8. The _____ _____ reports how well a business performs for a period of time.
9. The _____ _____ _____ _____ is a report that shows changes in capital.
10. The ending figure for capital from the statement of owner's equity is placed on the _____ _____.

Part II Instructions

Answer true or false to the following statements.

1. Accounts Receivable is a liability.
2. Liabilities produce revenue.
3. Revenue is an asset.
4. Capital means cash.
5. Bookkeeping is 50% of accounting.
6. The balance sheet lists assets, revenue, and owner's equity.
7. The balance sheet shows where we are now for a specific period of time.
8. Revenue creates an outward flow of assets.
9. Expenses are a subdivision of owner's equity.
10. Withdrawals are the only subdivision of owner's equity.
11. Withdrawals are listed on the income statement.
12. Revenue is a subdivision of owner's equity.
13. Revenues and withdrawals are listed on the income statement.
14. The income statement helps update the statement of owner's equity, and the statement of owner's equity helps update the balance sheet.
15. Withdrawals are listed on the statement of owner's equity.

Name _____ Class _____ Date _____

Part III Instructions

In column B, record the appropriate code(s) that result from recording the transaction in column A.

1. Increase in assets
2. Decrease in assets
3. Increase in liabilities
4. Decrease in liabilities
5. Increase in capital
6. Increase in revenues
7. Increase in expenses
8. Increase in withdrawals

	COLUMN A	COLUMN B
1.	EXAMPLE: Pete Smith invested $5,000 in his business.	1,5
2.	Bought computer equipment on account for $600.	
3.	Paid salaries of $70.	
4.	Bought additional computer equipment for $750 cash.	
5.	Paid rent expense of $90.	
6.	Received $5,000 in cash from revenue earned.	
7.	Paid heat expense of $15.	
8.	Earned revenue of $500 that will not be received until next month.	
9.	Paid amount owed on equipment previously purchased on account.	
10.	Paid for cleaning supplies expense, $15.	
11.	Customers paid $10 of amount previously owed.	
12.	Bought additional equipment of $1,000, half paid in cash and half charged.	
13.	Charged customer $100 for services performed.	
14.	Pete paid home phone bill from the company's cash.	
15.	Advertising expense incurred but not to be paid until next month.	

CHAPTER 1 SOLUTIONS TO SUMMARY PRACTICE TEST

Part I

1. The Sarbanes-Oxley Act
2. Assets
3. capital
4. balance sheet
5. Expenses
6. Cash
7. Withdrawals
8. income statement
9. statement of owner's equity
10. balance sheet

Part II

1. false
2. false
3. false
4. false
5. false
6. false
7. false
8. false
9. true
10. false
11. false
12. true
13. false
14. true
15. true

Part III

1. 1,5
2. 1,3
3. 7,2
4. 1,2
5. 7,2
6. 1,6
7. 7,2
8. 1,6
9. 4,2
10. 7,2
11. 1,2
12. 1,2,3
13. 1,6
14. 8,2
15. 7,3

Name _____ Class _____ Date _____

CONTINUING PROBLEM FOR CHAPTER 1

SANCHEZ COMPUTER CENTER

	ASSETS				=	LIABILITIES	+	OWNER'S EQUITY			
	Cash	+ Supplies	+ Computer Shop Equipment	+ Office Equipment	=	Accounts Payable	+	Freedman, Capital	− Freedman, Withdrawals	+ Revenue	− Expenses
a											
BALANCE											
b											
BALANCE											
c											
BALANCE											
d											
BALANCE											
e											
BALANCE											
f											
BALANCE											
g											
BALANCE											
h											
BALANCE											
i											
BALANCE											
j											
END BAL.											

SANCHEZ COMPUTER CENTER
INCOME STATEMENT
FOR THE MONTH ENDED JULY 31, 200X

SANCHEZ COMPUTER CENTER
STATEMENT OF OWNER'S EQUITY
FOR MONTH ENDED JULY 31, 200X

SANCHEZ COMPUTER CENTER
BALANCE SHEET
JULY 31, 200X

ASSETS | LIABILITIES AND OWNER'S EQUITY

Debits and Credits: Analyzing and Recording Business Transactions

SELF-REVIEW QUIZ 2-1

1. _____   4. _____
2. _____   5. _____
3. _____

SELF-REVIEW QUIZ 2-2

A.

1. Accounts Affected	2. Category	3. ↑↓	4. Rules	5. T Account Update

B.

1. Accounts Affected	2. Category	3. ↑↓	4. Rules	5. T Account Update

Name _____ Class _____ Date _____

C. 1. Accounts Affected	2. Category	3. ↑↓	4. Rules	5. T Account Update			

D. 1. Accounts Affected	2. Category	3. ↑↓	4. Rules	5. T Account Update			

E. 1. Accounts Affected	2. Category	3. ↑↓	4. Rules	5. T Account Update			

Name _____ Class _____ Date _____

SELF-REVIEW QUIZ 2-3

Cash	111
4,500	300
2,000	100
1,000	1,200
300	1,300
	2,600

Accounts Payable	211
300	700

Salon Fees	411
	3,500
	1,000

Accounts Receivable	121
1,000	300

Pam Jay, Capital	311
	4,000

Rent Expense	511
1,200	

Salon Equipment	131
700	

Pam Jay, Withdrawals	321
100	

Salon Supplies Exp.	521
1,300	

Salaries Expense	531
2,600	

Name _____ Class _____ Date _____

(1)

_____
_____
_____

(2)

_____
_____
_____

SG-27

Name _____ Class _____ Date _____

(3)

(4)

SG-28

Name _____ Class _____ Date _____

FORMS FOR DEMONSTRATION PROBLEM

(1,2,3)

| Advertising Expense 511 | Gas Expense 512 | Salaries Expense 513 | Telephone Expense 514 |

| Accounts Payable 211 | Mel Free, Capital 311 | Mel Free, Withdrawals 312 | Delivery Fees Earned 411 |

| Cash 111 | Accounts Receivable 112 | Office Equipment 121 | Delivery Trucks 122 |

SG-29

Name _____ Class _____ Date _____

FORMS FOR DEMONSTRATION PROBLEM (CONTINUED)

(4)

MEL'S DELIVERY SERVICE
TRIAL BALANCE
JULY 31, 200X

	Dr.	Cr.

(5A)

MEL'S DELIVERY SERVICE
INCOME STATEMENT
FOR MONTH ENDED JULY 31, 200X

SG-30

Name _____ Class _____ Date _____

FORMS FOR DEMONSTRATION PROBLEM (CONCLUDED)

(5B)

MEL'S DELIVERY SERVICE
STATEMENT OF OWNER'S EQUITY
FOR MONTH ENDED JULY 31, 200X

(5C)

MEL'S DELIVERY SERVICE
BALANCE SHEET
JULY 31, 200X

ASSETS   LIABILITIES AND OWNER'S EQUITY

SG-31

Name _____ Class _____ Date _____

CHAPTER 2
FORMS FOR CLASSROOM DEMONSTRATION EXERCISES SET A OR SET B

1.

2. A. _____ _____ _____ _____
   B. _____ _____ _____ _____
   C. _____ _____ _____ _____
   D. _____ _____ _____ _____
   E. _____ _____ _____ _____
   F. _____ _____ _____ _____
   G. _____ _____ _____ _____

3.

4. _____   **5.** A. _____
   _____   B. _____
   _____   C. _____
   _____   D. _____
   _____   E. _____
   _____   F. _____
   _____   G. _____
   _____   H. _____
   _____   I. _____
   _____   J. _____
   _____   K. _____

SG-32

Name _____ Class _____ Date _____

FORMS FOR EXERCISES

2-1.

(blank lines)

2-2.

1. Accounts Affected	2. Category	3. ↑ ↓	4. Rules	5. T Account Update

2-3.

Account	Category	↑ ↓	Financial Statement

Name _____ Class _____ Date _____

EXERCISES (CONTINUED)

2-4.

	Dr.	Cr.
A.	8	1
B.		
C.		
D.		
E.		
F.		
G.		
H.		
I.		

2-5.

(1)

HALL'S CLEANERS
INCOME STATEMENT
FOR MONTH ENDED JULY 31, 200X

(2)

HALL'S CLEANERS
STATEMENT OF OWNER'S EQUITY
FOR MONTH ENDED JULY 31, 200X

SG-34

EXERCISES (CONCLUDED)

(3)

HALL'S CLEANERS
BALANCE SHEET
JULY 31, 200X

ASSETS			LIABILITIES AND OWNER'S EQUITY		

Name _____ Class _____ Date _____

END OF CHAPTER PROBLEMS

PROBLEM 2A-1 OR PROBLEM 2B-1

Accounts Affected	Category	Inc. Dec. ↑ ↓	Rules	T Account Update
A.				
B.				
C.				
D.				
E.				
F.				

SG-36

PROBLEM 2A-2 OR PROBLEM 2B-2

| Cash 111 | Bernie Pillows, Withdrawals 312 |

| Office Equipment 121 | Consulting Fees Earned 411 |

| Accounts Payable 211 | Advertising Expense 511 |

| Bernie Pillows, Capital 311 | Rent Expense 512 |

PROBLEM 2A-3 OR PROBLEM 2B-3

(A)

Cash 111	Accounts Payable 211	Fees Earned 411
Accounts Receivable 112	Barry Joy, Capital 311	Rent Expense 511
Office Equipment 121	Barry Joy, Withdrawals 312	Utilities Expense 512

(B)

BARRY'S CLEANING SERVICE
TRIAL BALANCE
MAY 31, 200X

	Dr.	Cr.

Name _____ Class _____ Date _____

PROBLEM 2A-4 OR PROBLEM 2B-4

(A)

GRACIE LANTZ, ATTORNEY AT LAW
INCOME STATEMENT
FOR MONTH ENDED MAY 31, 200X

(B)

GRACIE LANTZ, ATTORNEY AT LAW
STATEMENT OF OWNER'S EQUITY
FOR MONTH ENDED MAY 31, 200X

Name _____ Class _____ Date _____

PROBLEM 2A-4 OR PROBLEM 2B-4 (CONCLUDED)

(C)

GRACIE LANTZ, ATTORNEY AT LAW
BALANCE SHEET
MAY 31, 200X

ASSETS

LIABILITIES AND OWNER'S EQUITY

SG-40

Name _____ Class _____ Date _____

PROBLEM 2A-5 OR PROBLEM 2B-5
(1,2,3)

| Advertising Expense 511 | Gas Expense 512 | Salaries Expense 513 | Telephone Expense 514 |

| Accounts Payable 211 | A. Angel, Capital 311 | A. Angel, Withdrawals 312 | Delivery Fees Earned 411 |

| Cash 111 | Accounts Receivable 112 | Office Equipment 121 | Delivery Trucks 122 |

Name _____ Class _____ Date _____

PROBLEM 2A-5 OR PROBLEM 2-B5 (CONTINUED)
(4)

ANGEL'S DELIVERY SERVICE
TRIAL BALANCE
MARCH 31, 200X

		Dr.	Cr.

(5A)

ANGEL'S DELIVERY SERVICE
INCOME STATEMENT
FOR MONTH ENDED MARCH 31, 200X

Name _____ Class _____ Date _____

PROBLEM 2A-5 OR PROBLEM 2B-5 (CONCLUDED)

(5B)

ANGEL'S DELIVERY SERVICE
STATEMENT OF OWNER'S EQUITY
FOR MONTH ENDED MARCH 31, 200X

(5C)

ANGEL'S DELIVERY SERVICE
BALANCE SHEET
MARCH 31, 200X

ASSETS   LIABILITIES AND OWNER'S EQUITY

SG-43

Name _____ Class _____ Date _____

CHAPTER 2
SUMMARY PRACTICE TEST:
DEBITS AND CREDITS: ANALYZING AND RECORDING
BUSINESS TRANSACTIONS

Part I Instructions

Fill in the blank(s) to complete the statement.

1. Financial reports do not contain _____ or _____.
2. The right side of any T account is called the _____ _____.
3. Assets are increased by _____.
4. The process of balancing an account involves _____.
5. Transaction analysis charts are an aid in recording _____ _____.
6. The _____ _____ _____ indicates the names and numbering system of accounts.
7. A(n) _____ is a group of accounts.
8. A(n) _____ _____ is an informal report that lists accounts and their balances.
9. Withdrawals are increased by _____.
10. The income statement, statement of owner's equity, and balance sheet may be prepared from a(n) _____ _____.
11. Cash, Accounts Receivable, and Equipment are examples of _____.
12. Increasing expenses ultimately cause owner's equity to _____.
13. An increase in rent expense is a(n) _____ by the rules of debits and credits.
14. A debit to one asset and a credit to another asset for the same transaction reflect a(n) _____ in assets.
15. The category of accounts receivable is a(n) _____.

Part II Instructions

Bea Paul opened a shuttle service company. From the following chart of accounts, indicate in column B (by account number) which account (s) will be debited or credited as related to the transaction in column A.

Name _____ Class _____ Date _____

Chart of Accounts

ASSETS	LIABILITIES	EXPENSES
10 Cash	50 Accounts Payable	80 Advertising
20 Accounts Receivable		90 Gas
30 Equipment	OWNER'S EQUITY	100 Salaries
40 Shuttle Bus	60 B. Paul, Capital	110 Telephone
	62 B. Paul, Withdrawals	
	REVENUE	
	70 Taxi Fees Earned	

COLUMN A	COLUMN B	
	DEBIT(S)	CREDIT(S)
1. EXAMPLE: Bea Paul invested $40,000 in the shuttle service.	10	60
2. Purchased a shuttle bus on account for $25,000.		
3. Bought equipment on account for $3,000.		
4. Advertising bill received, but not paid until next month, $60.		
5. Bea paid home telephone bill from company checkbook, $20.		
6. Collected $100 in cash from daily shuttle fees earned.		
7. Customer charged a shuttle ride of $20.		
8. Received partial payment for Transaction #7 of $10.		
9. Paid business telephone bill, $32.		
10. Purchased additional equipment for cash, $550.		
11. Paid shuttle driver salaries of $150.		
12. Drove customer on account to local train station for $6.		
13. Received $5 from customer who hired a shuttle for ride across town.		
14. Collected from past charged revenue, $15.		
15. Bought office equipment on account for $110.		

Part III Instructions

Answer true or false to the following statements.

1. There are no debit and credit columns found on the three financial statements.
2. A trial balance could balance but be wrong.
3. Withdrawals are listed on the credit column of the trial balance.
4. Double entry bookkeeping results in a system where the sum of all the debits is equal to the sum of all the credits.
5. The ledger is numbered like a textbook.

6. Withdrawals are always increased by credits.
7. An expense could create a liability.
8. A shift in assets means the total of assets must change.
9. The rules of debit and credit are constantly changing.
10. The transaction analysis chart is a teaching device.
11. The chart of accounts makes locating and identifying accounts easier.
12. The left side of any account is a credit.
13. A debit means all accounts are decreasing.
14. Financial statements are prepared from a trial balance.
15. The statement of owner's equity is prepared before the income statement.
16. Liabilities increase by credits.
17. Footings aid in balancing accounts.
18. Withdrawals are listed on the income statement.
19. The balance sheet contains the old figure for capital.
20. Think of a credit as always meaning something good.

CHAPTER 2
SOLUTIONS TO SUMMARY PRACTICE TEST

Part I

1. debits/credits
2. credit side
3. debits
4. footings
5. business transactions
6. chart of accounts
7. ledger (general)
8. trial balance
9. debits
10. trial balance
11. assets
12. decrease
13. debit
14. shift
15. asset

Part II

	Debit	Credit		Debit	Credit		Debit	Credit
1.	10	60	6.	10	70	11.	100	10
2.	40	50	7.	20	70	12.	20	70
3.	30	50	8.	10	20	13.	10	70
4.	80	50	9.	110	10	14.	10	20
5.	62	10	10.	30	10	15.	30	50

Part III

1. true
2. true
3. false
4. true
5. false
6. false
7. true
8. false
9. false
10. true
11. true
12. false
13. false
14. true
15. false
16. true
17. true
18. false
19. false
20. false

CONTINUING PROBLEM FOR CHAPTER 2

Cash 1000	Accounts Receivable 1020	Supplies 1030	Computer Shop Equipment 1080
Bal. 3,850		Bal. 250	Bal. 1,200

Freedman, Withdrawals 3010	Office Equipment 1090	Accounts Payable 2000	Freedman, Capital 3000
Bal. 100	Bal. 600	335 Bal.	4,500 Bal.

Utilities Expense 5030	Service Revenue 4000	Advertising Expense 5010	Rent Expense 5020
Bal. 85	1,650 Bal.		Bal. 400

Postage Expense 5070	Phone Expense 5040	Supplies Expense 5050	Insurance Expense 5060

Name _____ Class _____ Date _____

SANCHEZ COMPUTER CENTER
TRIAL BALANCE
AUGUST 31, 200X

Dr. Cr.

SANCHEZ COMPUTER CENTER
INCOME STATEMENT
FOR THE TWO MONTHS ENDED AUGUST 31, 200X

Name _____ Class _____ Date _____

SANCHEZ COMPUTER CENTER
STATEMENT OF OWNER'S EQUITY
FOR THE TWO MONTHS ENDED AUGUST 31, 200X

SANCHEZ COMPUTER CENTER
BALANCE SHEET
AUGUST 31, 200X

ASSETS   LIABILITIES AND OWNER'S EQUITY

Beginning the Accounting Cycle: Journalizing, Posting, and the Trial Balance

3

SELF-REVIEW QUIZ 3-1

LOWE'S REPAIR SERVICE
GENERAL JOURNAL

PAGE 1

Date	Account Titles and Description	PR	Dr.	Cr.

SG-50

Name _____ Class _____ Date _____

LOWE'S REPAIR SERVICE
GENERAL JOURNAL

PAGE 1 (Cont.)

Date	Account Titles and Description	PR	Dr.	Cr.

SELF-REVIEW QUIZ 3-2

CLARK'S WORD PROCESSING SERVICES
GENERAL JOURNAL

PAGE 1

Date 200X		Account Titles and Description	PR	Dr.	Cr.
May	1	Cash		10 000 00	
		Brenda Clark, Capital			10 000 00
		Initial investment of cash by owner			
	1	Word Processing Equipment		6 000 00	
		Cash			1 000 00
		Accounts Payable			5 000 00
		Purchase of equip. from Ben Co.			
	1	Prepaid Rent		1 200 00	
		Cash			1 200 00
		Rent paid in advance (3 months)			
	3	Office Supplies		600 00	
		Accounts Payable			600 00
		Purchase of supplies on acct. from Norris			
	7	Cash		3 000 00	
		Word Processing Fees			3 000 00
		Cash received for services rendered			
	13	Office Salaries Expense		650 00	
		Cash			650 00
		Payment of office salaries			
	18	Advertising Expense		250 00	
		Accounts Payable			250 00
		Bill received but not paid from Al's News			
	20	Brenda Clark, Withdrawals		625 00	
		Cash			625 00
		Personal withdrawal of cash			
	22	Accounts Receivable		5 000 00	
		Word Processing Fees			5 000 00
		Billed Morris Co. for fees earned			

CLARK'S WORD PROCESSING SERVICES
GENERAL JOURNAL

PAGE 2

Date 200X		Account Titles and Description	PR	Dr.	Cr.
May	27	Office Salaries Expense		650 00	
		Cash			650 00
		Payment of office salaries			
	28	Accounts Payable		2 500 00	
		Cash			2 500 00
		Paid half the amount owed Ben Co.			
	29	Telephone Expense		220 00	
		Cash			220 00
		Paid telephone bill			

SG-53

Name _____ Class _____ Date _____

PARTIAL LEDGER OF CLARK'S WORD PROCESSING SERVICE

CASH   **ACCOUNT NO. 111**

Date	Explanation	Post Ref.	Debit	Credit	Balance Debit	Balance Credit

ACCOUNTS RECEIVABLE   **ACCOUNT NO. 112**

Date	Explanation	Post Ref.	Debit	Credit	Balance Debit	Balance Credit

OFFICE SUPPLIES   ACCOUNT NO. 114

Date	Explanation	Post Ref.	Debit	Credit	Balance Debit	Balance Credit

PREPAID RENT   ACCOUNT NO. 115

Date	Explanation	Post Ref.	Debit	Credit	Balance Debit	Balance Credit

WORD PROCESSING EQUIPMENT   ACCOUNT NO. 121

Date	Explanation	Post Ref.	Debit	Credit	Balance Debit	Balance Credit

ACCOUNTS PAYABLE   ACCOUNT NO. 211

Date	Explanation	Post Ref.	Debit	Credit	Balance Debit	Balance Credit

Name _____ Class _____ Date _____

BRENDA CLARK, CAPITAL — ACCOUNT NO. 311

Date	Explanation	Post Ref.	Debit	Credit	Balance Debit	Balance Credit

BRENDA CLARK, WITHDRAWALS — ACCOUNT NO. 312

Date	Explanation	Post Ref.	Debit	Credit	Balance Debit	Balance Credit

WORD PROCESSING FEES — ACCOUNT NO. 411

Date	Explanation	Post Ref.	Debit	Credit	Balance Debit	Balance Credit

OFFICE SALARIES EXPENSE — ACCOUNT NO. 511

Date	Explanation	Post Ref.	Debit	Credit	Balance Debit	Balance Credit

Name _____ Class _____ Date _____

ADVERTISING EXPENSE   **ACCOUNT NO. 512**

Date	Explanation	Post Ref.	Debit	Credit	Balance Debit	Balance Credit

TELEPHONE EXPENSE   **ACCOUNT NO. 513**

Date	Explanation	Post Ref.	Debit	Credit	Balance Debit	Balance Credit

SELF-REVIEW QUIZ 3-3

1.

GENERAL JOURNAL

2.

PAGE 4

Date	Account Titles and Description	PR	Dr.	Cr.

Name _____ Class _____ Date _____

FORMS FOR DEMONSTRATION PROBLEM
(A, B)

ABBY'S EMPLOYMENT AGENCY
GENERAL JOURNAL

PAGE 1

Date	Account Titles and Description	PR	Dr.	Cr.

Name _____ Class _____ Date _____

FORMS FOR DEMONSTRATION PROBLEM (CONTINUED)

GENERAL LEDGER OF ABBY'S EMPLOYMENT AGENCY

CASH   **ACCOUNT NO. 111**

Date	Explanation	Post Ref.	Debit	Credit	Balance Debit	Balance Credit

ACCOUNTS RECEIVABLE   **ACCOUNT NO. 112**

Date	Explanation	Post Ref.	Debit	Credit	Balance Debit	Balance Credit

SUPPLIES   **ACCOUNT NO. 131**

Date	Explanation	Post Ref.	Debit	Credit	Balance Debit	Balance Credit

EQUIPMENT   **ACCOUNT NO. 141**

Date	Explanation	Post Ref.	Debit	Credit	Balance Debit	Balance Credit

Name _____ Class _____ Date _____

FORMS FOR DEMONSTRATION PROBLEM (CONTINUED)

ACCOUNTS PAYABLE   ACCOUNT NO. <u>211</u>

Date	Explanation	Post Ref.	Debit	Credit	Balance Debit	Balance Credit

A. TODD, CAPITAL   ACCOUNT NO. <u>311</u>

Date	Explanation	Post Ref.	Debit	Credit	Balance Debit	Balance Credit

A. TODD, WITHDRAWALS   ACCOUNT NO. <u>321</u>

Date	Explanation	Post Ref.	Debit	Credit	Balance Debit	Balance Credit

EMPLOYMENT FEES EARNED   ACCOUNT NO. <u>411</u>

Date	Explanation	Post Ref.	Debit	Credit	Balance Debit	Balance Credit

Name _____ Class _____ Date _____

FORMS FOR DEMONSTRATION PROBLEM (CONTINUED)

WAGE EXPENSE — ACCOUNT NO. **511**

Date	Explanation	Post Ref.	Debit	Credit	Balance Debit	Balance Credit

TELEPHONE EXPENSE — ACCOUNT NO. **521**

Date	Explanation	Post Ref.	Debit	Credit	Balance Debit	Balance Credit

ADVERTISING EXPENSE — ACCOUNT NO. **531**

Date	Explanation	Post Ref.	Debit	Credit	Balance Debit	Balance Credit

Name _____ Class _____ Date _____

FORMS FOR DEMONSTRATION PROBLEM (CONCLUDED)

ABBY'S EMPLOYMENT AGENCY
TRIAL BALANCE
MARCH 31, 200X

		Dr.	Cr.

Name _____ Class _____ Date _____

CHAPTER 3
FORMS FOR CLASSROOM DEMONSTRATION EXERCISES SET A OR SET B

1.
- A. _____
- B. _____
- C. _____
- D. _____
- E. _____
- F. _____
- G. _____
- H. _____
- I. _____

2.
- A. _____
- B. _____
- C. _____

3.

CASH   ACCOUNT NO. <u>111</u>

Date	Explanation	Post Ref.	Debit	Credit	Balance Debit	Balance Credit

_____

_____

4.

LEE CO.
TRIAL BALANCE
OCTOBER 31, 200X

	Dr.	Cr.

FORMS FOR CLASSROOM DEMONSTRATION EXERCISES SET A OR SET B (CONCLUDED)

5.

Date	Account Titles and Description	PR	Dr.	Cr.

FORMS FOR EXERCISES

3-1.

Date	Account Titles and Description	PR	Dr.	Cr.

EXERCISES (CONTINUED)

3-2.

Date	Account Titles and Description	PR	Dr.	Cr.

EXERCISES (CONTINUED)

3-3.

Date		Account Titles and Description	PR	Dr.	Cr.
200X					
April	6	Cash		15 000 —	
		A. King, Capital			15 000 —
		Cash investment			
	14	Equipment		9 000 —	
		Cash			4 000 —
		Accounts Payable			5 000 —
		Purchase of Equipment			

CASH ACCOUNT NO. 111

Date	Explanation	Post Ref.	Debit	Credit	Balance Debit	Balance Credit

EQUIPMENT ACCOUNT NO. 121

Date	Explanation	Post Ref.	Debit	Credit	Balance Debit	Balance Credit

ACCOUNTS PAYABLE ACCOUNT NO. 211

Date	Explanation	Post Ref.	Debit	Credit	Balance Debit	Balance Credit

A. KING, CAPITAL ACCOUNT NO. 311

Date	Explanation	Post Ref.	Debit	Credit	Balance Debit	Balance Credit

EXERCISES (CONTINUED)

3-4.
(A) PAGE 1

Date	Account Titles and Description	PR	Dr.	Cr.

(B)

CASH ACCOUNT NO. 111

Date	Explanation	Post Ref.	Debit	Credit	Balance Debit	Balance Credit

ACCOUNTS RECEIVABLE ACCOUNT NO. 112

Date	Explanation	Post Ref.	Debit	Credit	Balance Debit	Balance Credit

EXERCISES (CONTINUED)

EQUIPMENT   ACCOUNT NO. 121

Date	Explanation	Post Ref.	Debit	Credit	Balance Debit	Balance Credit

ACCOUNTS PAYABLE   ACCOUNT NO. 211

Date	Explanation	Post Ref.	Debit	Credit	Balance Debit	Balance Credit

J. LOWE, CAPITAL   ACCOUNT NO. 311

Date	Explanation	Post Ref.	Debit	Credit	Balance Debit	Balance Credit

J. LOWE, WITHDRAWALS   ACCOUNT NO. 312

Date	Explanation	Post Ref.	Debit	Credit	Balance Debit	Balance Credit

FEES EARNED   ACCOUNT NO. 411

Date	Explanation	Post Ref.	Debit	Credit	Balance Debit	Balance Credit

SALARIES EXPENSE   ACCOUNT NO. 511

Date	Explanation	Post Ref.	Debit	Credit	Balance Debit	Balance Credit

Name _____ Class _____ Date _____

EXERCISES (CONCLUDED)

(C)

LOWE COMPANY
TRIAL BALANCE
JULY 31, 200X

		Dr.	Cr.

3-5.

SUNG CO.
TRIAL BALANCE
MARCH 31, 200X

		Dr.	Cr.

3-6.

		Dr.	Cr.

SG-70

Name _____ Class _____ Date _____

END OF CHAPTER PROBLEMS

PROBLEM 3A-1 OR PROBLEM 3B-1

JACK'S CLEANING SERVICE
GENERAL JOURNAL

PAGE 1

Date	Account Titles and Description	PR	Dr.	Cr.

Name _____ Class _____ Date _____

PROBLEM 3A-1 OR PROBLEM 3B-1 (CONCLUDED)

JACK'S CLEANING SERVICE
GENERAL JOURNAL

PAGE 2

Date	Account Titles and Description	PR	Dr.	Cr.

Name _____ Class _____ Date _____

PROBLEM 3A-2 OR PROBLEM 3B-2
(A, B)

BETTY'S ART STUDIO
GENERAL JOURNAL

PAGE 1

Date	Account Titles and Description	PR	Dr.	Cr.

SG-73

Name _____ Class _____ Date _____

PROBLEM 3A-2 OR PROBLEM 3B-2 (CONTINUED)

GENERAL LEDGER OF BETTY'S ART STUDIO

CASH   **ACCOUNT NO. 111**

Date	Explanation	Post Ref.	Debit	Credit	Balance Debit	Balance Credit

ACCOUNTS RECEIVABLE   **ACCOUNT NO. 112**

Date	Explanation	Post Ref.	Debit	Credit	Balance Debit	Balance Credit

PREPAID RENT   **ACCOUNT NO. 114**

Date	Explanation	Post Ref.	Debit	Credit	Balance Debit	Balance Credit

ART SUPPLIES   **ACCOUNT NO. 121**

Date	Explanation	Post Ref.	Debit	Credit	Balance Debit	Balance Credit

PROBLEM 3A-2 OR PROBLEM 3B-2 (CONTINUED)

EQUIPMENT — ACCOUNT NO. 131

Date	Explanation	Post Ref.	Debit	Credit	Balance Debit	Balance Credit

ACCOUNTS PAYABLE — ACCOUNT NO. 211

Date	Explanation	Post Ref.	Debit	Credit	Balance Debit	Balance Credit

BETTY RICE, CAPITAL — ACCOUNT NO. 311

Date	Explanation	Post Ref.	Debit	Credit	Balance Debit	Balance Credit

BETTY RICE, WITHDRAWALS — ACCOUNT NO. 312

Date	Explanation	Post Ref.	Debit	Credit	Balance Debit	Balance Credit

PROBLEM 3A-2 OR PROBLEM 3B-2 (CONTINUED)

ART FEES EARNED   **ACCOUNT NO. 411**

Date	Explanation	Post Ref.	Debit	Credit	Balance Debit	Balance Credit

ELECTRICAL EXPENSE   **ACCOUNT NO. 511**

Date	Explanation	Post Ref.	Debit	Credit	Balance Debit	Balance Credit

SALARIES EXPENSE   **ACCOUNT NO. 521**

Date	Explanation	Post Ref.	Debit	Credit	Balance Debit	Balance Credit

TELEPHONE EXPENSE   **ACCOUNT NO. 531**

Date	Explanation	Post Ref.	Debit	Credit	Balance Debit	Balance Credit

Name _____ Class _____ Date _____

PROBLEM 3A-2 OR PROBLEM 3B-2 (CONCLUDED)

(C)

BETTY'S ART STUDIO
TRIAL BALANCE
JUNE 30, 200X

	Dr.	Cr.

Name _____ Class _____ Date _____

PROBLEM 3A-3 OR PROBLEM 3B-3
(A, B)

A. FRENCH'S PLACEMENT AGENCY
GENERAL JOURNAL

PAGE 1

Date	Account Titles and Description	PR	Dr.	Cr.

Name _____ Class _____ Date _____

PROBLEM 3A-3 OR PROBLEM 3B-3 (CONTINUED)

GENERAL LEDGER OF A. FRENCH'S PLACEMENT AGENCY

CASH   **ACCOUNT NO. 111**

Date	Explanation	Post Ref.	Debit	Credit	Balance Debit	Balance Credit

ACCOUNTS RECEIVABLE   **ACCOUNT NO. 112**

Date	Explanation	Post Ref.	Debit	Credit	Balance Debit	Balance Credit

SUPPLIES   **ACCOUNT NO. 131**

Date	Explanation	Post Ref.	Debit	Credit	Balance Debit	Balance Credit

EQUIPMENT   **ACCOUNT NO. 141**

Date	Explanation	Post Ref.	Debit	Credit	Balance Debit	Balance Credit

Name _____ Class _____ Date _____

PROBLEM 3A-3 OR PROBLEM 3B-3 (CONTINUED)

ACCOUNTS PAYABLE   **ACCOUNT NO. 211**

Date	Explanation	Post Ref.	Debit	Credit	Balance Debit	Balance Credit

A. FRENCH, CAPITAL   **ACCOUNT NO. 311**

Date	Explanation	Post Ref.	Debit	Credit	Balance Debit	Balance Credit

A. FRENCH, WITHDRAWALS   **ACCOUNT NO. 312**

Date	Explanation	Post Ref.	Debit	Credit	Balance Debit	Balance Credit

PLACEMENT FEES EARNED   **ACCOUNT NO. 411**

Date	Explanation	Post Ref.	Debit	Credit	Balance Debit	Balance Credit

PROBLEM 3A-3 OR PROBLEM 3B-3 (CONTINUED)

WAGE EXPENSE   **ACCOUNT NO. 511**

Date	Explanation	Post Ref.	Debit	Credit	Balance Debit	Balance Credit

TELEPHONE EXPENSE   **ACCOUNT NO. 521**

Date	Explanation	Post Ref.	Debit	Credit	Balance Debit	Balance Credit

ADVERTISING EXPENSE   **ACCOUNT NO. 531**

Date	Explanation	Post Ref.	Debit	Credit	Balance Debit	Balance Credit

PROBLEM 3A-3 OR PROBLEM 3B-3 (CONCLUDED)

(C)

A. FRENCH'S PLACEMENT AGENCY
TRIAL BALANCE
JUNE 30, 200X

Name _____ Class _____ Date _____

CHAPTER 3
SUMMARY PRACTICE TEST:
BEGINNING THE ACCOUNTING CYCLE: JOURNALIZING, POSTING, AND THE TRIAL BALANCE

Part I Instructions

Fill in the blank(s) to complete the statement.

1. A fiscal year runs for _____ months.
2. _____ _____ are prepared for parts of a fiscal year (monthly, quarterly, etc.).
3. The _____ _____ _____ eliminates the need for footings.
4. The positive balance of each account is referred to as its _____ _____.
5. The process of recording transactions in a journal is called _____.
6. Entries are journalized in _____ _____.
7. A ledger is often called a(n) _____ _____ _____ _____ .
8. The _____ portion of a journal entry is indented and placed below the _____ portion.
9. A journal entry requiring three or more accounts is called a(n) _____ _____ .
10. Accounts receivable is a(n) _____ on the balance sheet.
11. When supplies are used up or consumed they become a(n) _____.
12. The book of original entry usually refers to a(n) _____.
13. The process of transferring information from a journal to a ledger is called _____.
14. _____ _____ deals with the process of updating the PR of the journal from the account number of the ledger to indicate to which account in the ledger information has been posted.
15. Recording $995.00 as $99.50 is an example of a(n) _____.

Name _____ Class _____ Date _____

Part II Instructions

Match the term in column A to the definition, example, or phrase in column B. Be sure to use a letter only once.

COLUMN A

_g_ 1. EXAMPLE: Book of original entry
____ 2. Non-Business Expense
____ 3. Slide
____ 4. Transposition
____ 5. Posting
____ 6. General Journal
____ 7. Cross-reference
____ 8. Journalizing
____ 9. Balance Sheet prepared monthly
____ 10. A fiscal year

COLUMN B

a. 243 — 2430
b. Transferring information from a general journal to a ledger
c. Chronological order
d. Increased by a credit
e. Withdrawal
f. Compound journal entry
g. General journal
h. Rearrangement of digits of a number by accident
i. Updating PR column of journal from ledger account
j. Trial balance
k. Place to record transactions
l. Accounting cycle
m. Accounting period
n. Interim statements

Part III Instructions

Answer true or false to the following statements.

1. A slide cannot affect position of numbers.
2. The totals of a trial balance may possibly not balance due to transpositions.
3. Withdrawals has a normal balance of a credit.
4. The running balance of an account can be kept in a four-column account.
5. The journal links debits and credits in alphabetical order.
6. The ledger accumulates information from the journal.
7. The post reference column of a ledger records the account number of that account.
8. An accounting cycle must be from January 1 to December 31.
9. The ledger is the book of original entry.
10. The income statement is prepared for a specific accounting period.
11. Interim statements are prepared for an entire fiscal year.
12. A calendar year could be a fiscal year.
13. 390 written by mistake as 3,900 is an example of a slide.

14. If the totals of a trial balance balance, the individual balance of items must be correct.
15. The equality of debits and credits on a trial balance does not guarantee that transactions have been properly recorded.
16. The trial balance is prepared from the journal.
17. Cross-referencing means never updating the post reference column of the journal.
18. Journals and ledgers are always in the same book.
19. The normal balance of each account is located on the same side that increases the acccount.
20. Ruling of four-column accounts is eliminated.

CHAPTER 3
SOLUTIONS TO SUMMARY PRACTICE TEST

Part I

1. 12
2. Interim statements
3. four-column ledger
4. normal balance
5. journalizing
6. chronological order
7. book of final entry
8. credit, debit
9. compound journal entry
10. asset
11. expense
12. journal
13. posting
14. Cross-reference
15. slide

Part II

1. g
2. e
3. a
4. h
5. b
6. k
7. i
8. c
9. n
10. m

Part III

1. false
2. true
3. false
4. true
5. false
6. true
7. false
8. false
9. false
10. true
11. false
12. true
13. true
14. false
15. true
16. false
17. false
18. false
19. true
20. true

CONTINUING PROBLEM FOR CHAPTER 3

SANCHEZ COMPUTER CENTER
GENERAL JOURNAL

PAGE 1

Date	Account Titles and Description	PR	Dr.	Cr.

SANCHEZ COMPUTER CENTER
GENERAL JOURNAL

PAGE 1 (Cont.)

Date	Account Titles and Description	PR	Dr.	Cr.

Name _____ Class _____ Date _____

CASH   **ACCOUNT NO. 1000**

Date		Explanation	Post Ref.	Debit	Credit	Balance Debit	Balance Credit
9/1	0X	Balance forward	✔			2 865 00	

SG-88

Name _____ Class _____ Date _____

ACCOUNTS RECEIVABLE   ACCOUNT NO. 1020

Date		Explanation	Post Ref.	Debit	Credit	Balance Debit	Balance Credit
9/1	0X	Balance forward	✔			850 00	

PREPAID RENT   ACCOUNT NO. 1025

Date	Explanation	Post Ref.	Debit	Credit	Balance Debit	Balance Credit

SUPPLIES   ACCOUNT NO. 1030

Date		Explanation	Post Ref.	Debit	Credit	Balance Debit	Balance Credit
9/1	0X	Balance forward	✔			450 00	

COMPUTER SHOP EQUIPMENT   ACCOUNT NO. 1080

Date		Explanation	Post Ref.	Debit	Credit	Balance Debit	Balance Credit
9/1	0X		✔			1200 00	

OFFICE EQUIPMENT ACCOUNT NO. 1090

Date	Explanation	Post Ref.	Debit	Credit	Balance Debit	Balance Credit
9/1 0X	Balance forward	✔			600 00	

ACCOUNTS PAYABLE ACCOUNT NO. 2000

Date	Explanation	Post Ref.	Debit	Credit	Balance Debit	Balance Credit
9/1 0X	Balance forward	✔				405 00

FREEDMAN, CAPITAL ACCOUNT NO. 3000

Date	Explanation	Post Ref.	Debit	Credit	Balance Debit	Balance Credit
9/1 0X	Balance forward	✔				450 00

FREEDMAN, WITHDRAWALS ACCOUNT NO. 3010

Date	Explanation	Post Ref.	Debit	Credit	Balance Debit	Balance Credit
9/1 0X	Balance forward	✔			100 00	

Name _____ Class _____ Date _____

SERVICE REVENUE   ACCOUNT NO. 4000

Date		Explanation	Post Ref.	Debit	Credit	Balance Debit	Balance Credit
9/1	0X	Balance forward	✓				3 400 00

ADVERTISING EXPENSE   ACCOUNT NO. 5010

Date		Explanation	Post Ref.	Debit	Credit	Balance Debit	Balance Credit
9/1	0X	Balance forward	✓			1 400 00	

RENT EXPENSE   ACCOUNT NO. 5020

Date		Explanation	Post Ref.	Debit	Credit	Balance Debit	Balance Credit
9/1	0X	Balance forward	✓			400 00	

UTILITIES EXPENSE — ACCOUNT NO. 5030

Date		Explanation	Post Ref.	Debit	Credit	Balance Debit	Balance Credit
9/1	0X	Balance forward	✔			8 5 00	

PHONE EXPENSE — ACCOUNT NO. 5040

Date		Explanation	Post Ref.	Debit	Credit	Balance Debit	Balance Credit
9/1	0X	Balance forward	✔			1 5 5 00	

SUPPLIES EXPENSE — ACCOUNT NO. 5050

Date	Explanation	Post Ref.	Debit	Credit	Balance Debit	Balance Credit

Name _____ Class _____ Date _____

INSURANCE EXPENSE   ACCOUNT NO. 5060

Date	Explanation	Post Ref.	Debit	Credit	Balance Debit	Balance Credit
9/1 0X	Balance forward	✓			1 50 00	

POSTAGE EXPENSE   ACCOUNT NO. 5070

Date	Explanation	Post Ref.	Debit	Credit	Balance Debit	Balance Credit
9/1 0X	Balance forward	✓			50 00	

Name _____ Class _____ Date _____

SANCHEZ COMPUTER CENTER
TRIAL BALANCE
SEPTEMBER 30, 200X

	Dr.	Cr.

SANCHEZ COMPUTER CENTER
INCOME STATEMENT
FOR THE QUARTER ENDED 9/30/0X

SANCHEZ COMPUTER CENTER
STATEMENT OF OWNER'S EQUITY
FOR THE QUARTER ENDED 9/30/0X

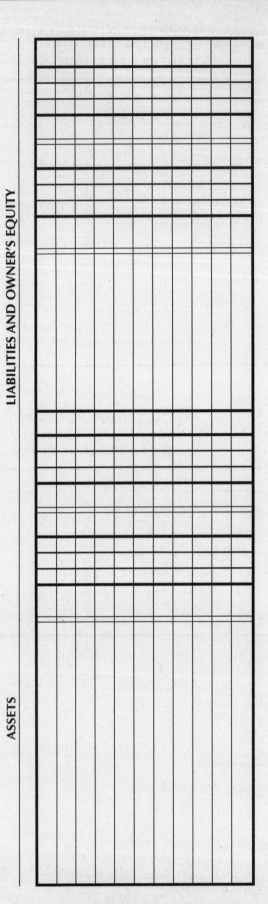

4 The Accounting Cycle Continued: Preparing Worksheets and Financial Statements

SELF-REVIEW QUIZ 4-1

Use one of the blank fold-out worksheets that accompanied your textbook.

Name _____ Class _____ Date _____

SELF-REVIEW QUIZ 4-2

(1) _____

(2) _____

LIABILITIES AND OWNER'S EQUITY

ASSETS

Name _____ Class _____ Date _____

FORMS FOR DEMONSTRATION PROBLEM

(1)
Use one of the blank fold-out worksheets that accompanied your textbook.

(2)

FROST COMPANY
INCOME STATEMENT
FOR MONTH ENDED DECEMBER 31, 200X

(2)

FROST COMPANY
STATEMENT OF OWNER'S EQUITY
FOR MONTH ENDED DECEMBER 31, 200X

DEMONSTRATION PROBLEM (CONCLUDED)

(2)

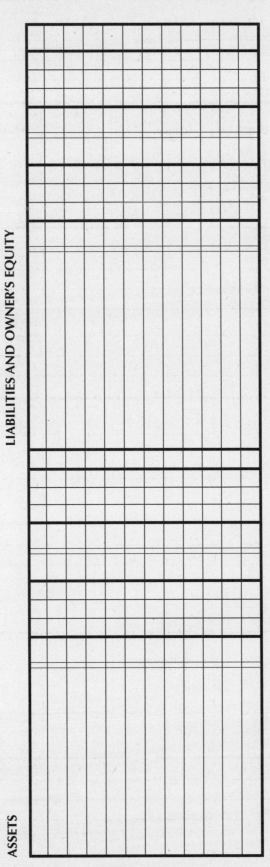

Name _____ Class _____ Date _____

CHAPTER 4
FORMS FOR CLASSROOM DEMONSTRATION EXERCISES SET A OR SET B

1. A. _____

B.

1. Accounts Affected	2. Category	3. ↑ ↓	4. Rules	5. T Account

C. _____

2. A. _____

B.

1. Accounts Affected	2. Category	3. ↑ ↓	4. Rules	5. T Account

C. _____

3. A. _____
B. _____
C.

1. Accounts Affected	2. Category	3. ↑ ↓	4. Rules	5. T Account

D. _____

SG-102

Name _____ Class _____ Date _____

4. A.

1. Accounts Affected	2. Category	3. ↑ ↓	4. Rules	5. T Account

B. _____
_____

5.
A. _____ H. _____
B. _____ I. _____
C. _____ J. _____
D. _____ K. _____
E. _____ L. _____
F. _____ M. _____
G. _____ N. _____

6.

A. _____
_____
_____

B. _____
_____
_____
_____

SG-103

Name _____ Class _____ Date _____

FORMS FOR EXERCISES

4-1.

Account	Category	Normal Balance	Financial Statement(s) Found on

4-2.

Accounts Affected	Category	↑ ↓	Rules	Amount
A.				
B.				

4-3.

A. _____

B. _____

4-4.

Use one of the blank fold-out worksheets that accompanied your textbook.

SG-104

Name _____ Class _____ Date _____

EXERCISES (CONTINUED)

4-5.
(A)

J. TRENT
INCOME STATEMENT
FOR MONTH ENDED DECEMBER 31, 200X

(B)

J. TRENT
STATEMENT OF OWNER'S EQUITY
FOR MONTH ENDED DECEMBER 31, 200X

EXERCISES (CONCLUDED)
(C)

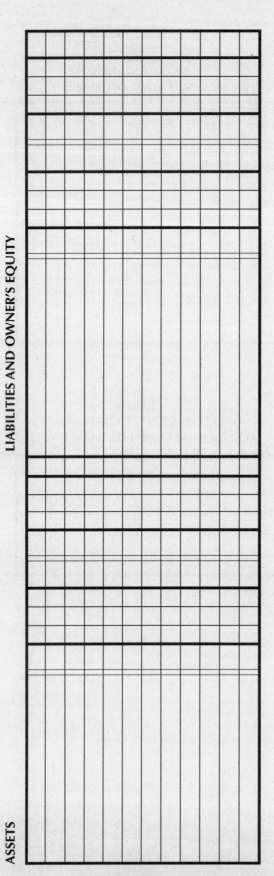

Name _____ Class _____ Date _____

END OF CHAPTER PROBLEMS

PROBLEM 4A-1 OR PROBLEM 4B-1

Use one of the blank fold-out worksheets that accompanied your textbook.

PROBLEM 4A-2 OR PROBLEM 4B-2

Use one of the blank fold-out worksheets that accompanied your textbook.

PROBLEM 4A-3 OR PROBLEM 4B-3

Use one of the blank fold-out worksheets that accompanied your textbook.

(2)

KEVIN'S MOVING CO.
INCOME STATEMENT
FOR MONTH ENDED OCTOBER 31, 200X

KEVIN'S MOVING CO.
STATEMENT OF OWNER'S EQUITY
FOR MONTH ENDED OCTOBER 31, 200X

(2)

SG-107

PROBLEM 4A-3 OR PROBLEM 4B-3 (CONCLUDED)

(2)

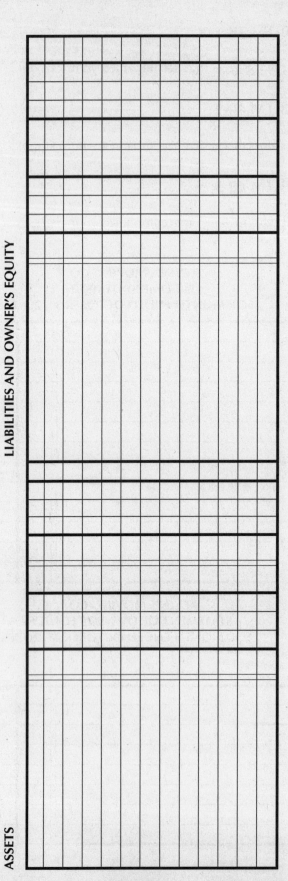

SG-108

PROBLEM 4A-4 OR PROBLEM 4B-4

Use one of the blank fold-out worksheets that accompanied your textbook.

(2)

DICK'S REPAIR SERVICE
INCOME STATEMENT
FOR MONTH ENDED NOVEMBER 30, 200X

(2)

DICK'S REPAIR SERVICE
STATEMENT OF OWNER'S EQUITY
FOR MONTH ENDED NOVEMBER 30, 200X

Name_____ Class_____ Date_____

PROBLEM 4A-4 OR PROBLEM 4B-4 (CONCLUDED)

(2)

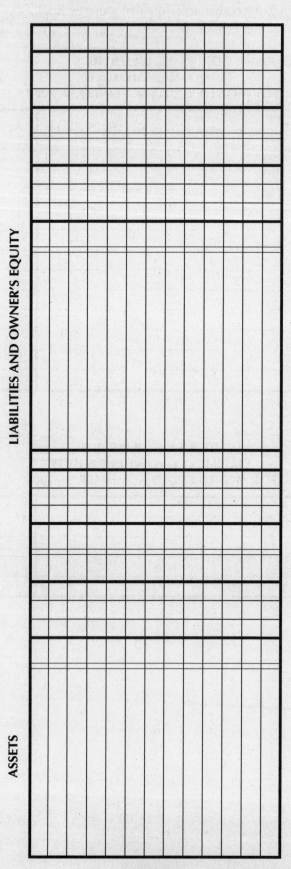

CHAPTER 4
SUMMARY PRACTICE TEST:
THE ACCOUNTING CYCLE CONTINUED:
PREPARING WORKSHEETS AND FINANCIAL STATEMENTS

Part I Instructions

Fill in the blank(s) to complete the statement.

1. _____ is an estimate.
2. A(n) _____ will decrease accumulated depreciation.
3. _____ affect both the income statement and balance sheet.
4. The adjustment for supplies reflects the amount of supplies _____ _____.
5. Supplies Expense is found on the income statement. Supplies are found on the _____ _____.
6. _____ _____ reflects the cost of equipment at time of purchase.
7. Depreciation Expense is found on the _____ _____.
8. _____ _____ is a contra asset that has a credit balance.
9. Accumulated Depreciation, a contra asset, is found on the _____ _____.
10. Historical or original cost of an auto less _____ _____ reflects the unused amount of the auto on the accounting books.
11. Withdrawals are found in the _____ column of the balance sheet section of the worksheet.
12. Salaries Payable is a liability that will appear in the _____ _____ _____ _____ of the worksheet.
13. The figure for net income on the worksheet is carried over to the _____ column of the balance sheet.
14. A worksheet is a(n) _____ report.
15. _____ _____ are prepared after the completion of the worksheet.

Part II Instructions

Complete the following statements by circling the letter of the appropriate answer.

SG-111

Name _____ Class _____ Date _____

1. The adjustment for depreciation results in Accumulated Depreciation
    a. decreasing.
    b. staying the same.
    c. increasing.
2. The historical or original cost of an asset on the worksheet
    a. never changes.
    b. sometimes changes.
    c. continually changes.
3. Net income on the worksheet is carried over to the
    a. trial balance.
    b. adjusted trial balance.
    c. balance sheet column.
4. Accumulated Depreciation is found on
    a. a worksheet.
    b. an income statement.
    c. both a worksheet and an income statement.
5. Accumulated Depreciation, a contra asset, is increased by a
    a. debit.
    b. credit.
    c. both a and b.
6. A worksheet is usually completed
    a. one column at a time.
    b. two columns at a time.
    c. three columns at a time.
7. Withdrawals on the worksheet are found in the
    a. debit column of the income statement.
    b. debit column of the balance sheet.
    c. both a and b.
8. The worksheet specifically shows the
    a. beginning figure for owner capital.
    b. ending figure for owner capital.
    c. average figure for owner capital.
9. The total of the assets on a formal balance sheet will _____ equal the total of the debit column of the balance sheet on the worksheet.
    a. always
    b. sometimes
    c. never
10. The adjustment for depreciation affects
    a. the income statement.
    b. the balance sheet.
    c. both a and b.
11. The adjustment for supplies requires one to know
    a. beginning supplies plus supplies purchased.
    b. supplies on hand.
    c. both a and b.

12. The purpose of adjustments is to
    a. bring general journals up to date.
    b. bring ledger accounts up to proper balances in the journal.
    c. bring ledger accounts to proper balance.
13. Book values equals cost less
    a. expenses.
    b. accumulated depreciation.
    c. neither a nor b.
14. The _____ is an informal report.
    a. income statement
    b. balance sheet
    c. worksheet

Part III Instructions

Answer true or false to the following statements.

1. The normal balance of accumulated depreciation is a credit.
2. Liabilities are only income statement accounts.
3. The total of the adjustments column may balance but be incorrect.
4. Prepaid rent is found on the income statement.
5. Rent expense is found on the income statement.
6. Debits and credits are found on financial statements.
7. Historical cost relates only to automobiles.
8. Accumulated Depreciation is found on the income statement.
9. As Accumulated Depreciation increases, the historical cost changes.
10. The adjustment for depreciation directly affects cash.
11. An expense is only recorded when it is paid.
12. The ending figure for owner capital does not have to be calculated from the worksheet.
13. Withdrawals have the same balance as Accumulated Depreciation.
14. Salaries Payable is an asset on the income statement.
15. Net loss would never be shown on a worksheet.
16. The net income on the worksheet is the same amount on the income statement.
17. Worksheets must use dollar signs.
18. The worksheet eliminates the need to prepare financial statements.
19. Cost less accumulated depreciation equals book value.
20. Accrued Salaries are expenses that have already been paid for.

CHAPTER 4
SOLUTIONS TO SUMMARY PRACTICE TEST

Part I

1. Depreciation
2. debit
3. Adjustments
4. used up
5. balance sheet
6. Historical (original) cost
7. income statement
8. Accumulated Depreciation
9. balance sheet
10. accumulated depreciation
11. debit
12. balance sheet credit column
13. credit
14. informal
15. Financial statements

Part II

1. c
2. a
3. c
4. a
5. b
6. b
7. b
8. a
9. c
10. c
11. c
12. c
13. b
14. c

Part III

1. true
2. false
3. true
4. false
5. true
6. false
7. false
8. false
9. false
10. false
11. false
12. true
13. false
14. false
15. false
16. true
17. false
18. false
19. true
20. false

Name _____ Class _____ Date _____

CONTINUING PROBLEM FOR CHAPTER 4*

SANCHEZ COMPUTER CENTER
INCOME STATEMENT
FOR THE THREE MONTHS ENDED SEPTEMBER 30, 200X

SANCHEZ COMPUTER CENTER
STATEMENT OF OWNER'S EQUITY
FOR THE THREE MONTHS ENDED SEPTEMBER 30, 200X

*Use one of the blank fold-out worksheets that accompanied your textbook.

Name _____ Class _____ Date _____

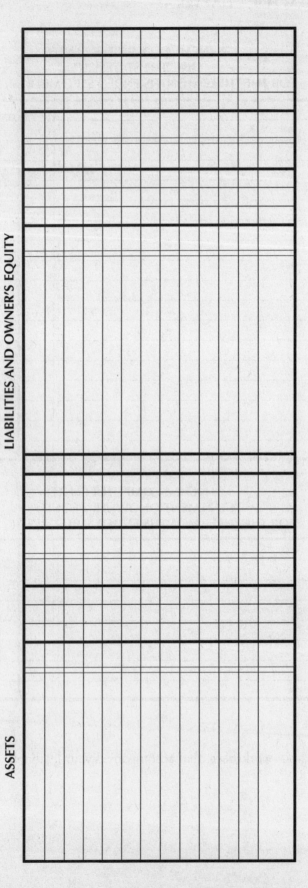

SG-116

5. The Accounting Cycle Completed: Adjusting, Closing, and the Post-Closing Trial Balance

SELF-REVIEW QUIZ 5-1

(1) PAGE 2

Date	Account Titles and Description	PR	Dr.	Cr.

(2) Partial Ledger

Depreciation Expense, Store Equipment 511	Accumulated Depreciation, Store Equipment 122
	4

Prepaid Insurance 116	Insurance Expense 516
3	

Store Supplies 114	Supplies Expense 514
5	

Salaries Expense 512	Salaries Payable 212
8	

SELF-REVIEW QUIZ 5-2
(1)

P. Logan, Capital 310	Revenue from Clients 410	Supplies Expense 514
14	25	4

P. Logan, Withdrawals 311	Depreciation Expense, Store Equipment 510	Insurance Expense 516
3	1	2

Income Summary 312	Salaries Expense 512	Rent Expense 518
	11	2

Name _____ Class _____ Date _____

(2) _____

SELF-REVIEW QUIZ 5-3

Name _____ Class _____ Date _____

FORMS FOR DEMONSTRATION PROBLEM

Use one of the blank fold-out worksheets that accompanied your textbook.

ROLO COMPANY
GENERAL JOURNAL

PAGE 1

Date	Account Titles and Description	PR	Dr.	Cr.

SG-121

FORMS FOR DEMONSTRATION PROBLEM (CONTINUED)

ROLO COMPANY
GENERAL JOURNAL

PAGE 2

Date	Account Titles and Description	PR	Dr.	Cr.

FORMS FOR DEMONSTRATION PROBLEM (CONTINUED)

CASH   **ACCOUNT NO. 111**

Date	Explanation	Post Ref.	Debit	Credit	Balance Debit	Balance Credit

ACCOUNTS RECEIVABLE   **ACCOUNT NO. 112**

Date	Explanation	Post Ref.	Debit	Credit	Balance Debit	Balance Credit

PREPAID RENT   **ACCOUNT NO. 114**

Date	Explanation	Post Ref.	Debit	Credit	Balance Debit	Balance Credit

OFFICE SUPPLIES   **ACCOUNT NO. 115**

Date	Explanation	Post Ref.	Debit	Credit	Balance Debit	Balance Credit

Name _____ Class _____ Date _____

FORMS FOR DEMONSTRATION PROBLEM (CONTINUED)

OFFICE EQUIPMENT ACCOUNT NO. <u>121</u>

Date	Explanation	Post Ref.	Debit	Credit	Balance Debit	Balance Credit

ACCUMULATED DEPRECIATION, OFFICE EQUIPMENT ACCOUNT NO. <u>122</u>

Date	Explanation	Post Ref.	Debit	Credit	Balance Debit	Balance Credit

ACCOUNTS PAYABLE ACCOUNT NO. <u>211</u>

Date	Explanation	Post Ref.	Debit	Credit	Balance Debit	Balance Credit

Name _____ Class _____ Date _____

FORMS FOR DEMONSTRATION PROBLEM (CONTINUED)

SALARIES PAYABLE ACCOUNT NO. **212**

Date	Explanation	Post Ref.	Debit	Credit	Balance Debit	Balance Credit

ROLO KERN, CAPITAL ACCOUNT NO. **311**

Date	Explanation	Post Ref.	Debit	Credit	Balance Debit	Balance Credit

ROLO KERN, WITHDRAWALS ACCOUNT NO. **312**

Date	Explanation	Post Ref.	Debit	Credit	Balance Debit	Balance Credit

INCOME SUMMARY ACCOUNT NO. **313**

Date	Explanation	Post Ref.	Debit	Credit	Balance Debit	Balance Credit

FEES EARNED ACCOUNT NO. **411**

Date	Explanation	Post Ref.	Debit	Credit	Balance Debit	Balance Credit

Name _____ Class _____ Date _____

FORMS FOR DEMONSTRATION PROBLEM (CONTINUED)

SALARIES EXPENSE   **ACCOUNT NO. 511**

Date	Explanation	Post Ref.	Debit	Credit	Balance Debit	Balance Credit

ADVERTISING EXPENSE   **ACCOUNT NO. 512**

Date	Explanation	Post Ref.	Debit	Credit	Balance Debit	Balance Credit

RENT EXPENSE   **ACCOUNT NO. 513**

Date	Explanation	Post Ref.	Debit	Credit	Balance Debit	Balance Credit

OFFICE SUPPLIES EXPENSE   **ACCOUNT NO. 514**

Date	Explanation	Post Ref.	Debit	Credit	Balance Debit	Balance Credit

DEPRECIATION EXPENSE, OFFICE EQUIPMENT   **ACCOUNT NO. 515**

Date	Explanation	Post Ref.	Debit	Credit	Balance Debit	Balance Credit

FORMS FOR DEMONSTRATION PROBLEM (CONTINUED)

ROLO COMPANY
INCOME STATEMENT
FOR MONTH ENDED JANUARY 31, 200X

ROLO COMPANY
STATEMENT OF OWNER'S EQUITY
FOR MONTH ENDED JANUARY 31, 200X

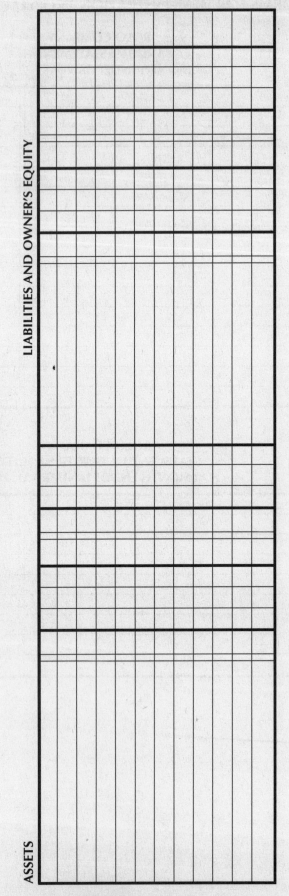

FORMS FOR DEMONSTRATION PROBLEM (CONCLUDED)

ROLO COMPANY
POST-CLOSING TRIAL BALANCE
JANUARY 31, 200X

CHAPTER 5
FORMS FOR CLASSROOM DEMONSTRATION EXERCISES SET A OR SET B

GENERAL JOURNAL

1.

PAGE 3

Date	Account Titles and Description	PR	Dr.	Cr.

Prepaid Insurance   115

Store Supplies   116

Accumulated Depreciation
Store Equipment   119

Salaries Payable   210

Insurance Expense   510

Depreciation Expense,
Store Equipment   512

Supplies Expense   514

Salaries Expense   516

2.

GENERAL JOURNAL

3.

PAGE 4

Date	Account Titles and Description	PR	Dr.	Cr.

4.

Income Summary   314

_____

5.

Mel Blanc, Capital   310

_____

FORMS FOR EXERCISES

5-1.

Date	Account Titles and Description	PR	Dr.	Cr.

5-2.

	TEMPORARY	PERMANENT	WILL BE CLOSED
1. Income Summary			
2. Jen Rich, Capital			
3. Salary Expense			
4. Jen Rich, Withdrawals			
5. Fees Earned			
6. Accounts Payable			
7. Cash			

EXERCISES (CONTINUED)

5-3.

Date	Account Titles and Description	PR	Dr.	Cr.

EXERCISES (CONCLUDED)

5-4.

Date	Account Titles and Description	PR	Dr.	Cr.

5-5.

WEY CO.
POST-CLOSING TRIAL BALANCE
DECEMBER 31, 200X

		Dr.	Cr.

Name _____ Class _____ Date _____

END OF CHAPTER PROBLEMS

PROBLEM 5A-1 OR PROBLEM 5B-1

Use one of the blank fold-out worksheets that accompanied your textbook.

(2)

DEBBIE'S DANCE STUDIO
GENERAL JOURNAL

PAGE 3

Date	Account Titles and Description	PR	Dr.	Cr.

Name _____ Class _____ Date _____

PROBLEM 5A-2 OR PROBLEM 5B-2

(1)

POTTER CLEANING SERVICE
GENERAL JOURNAL

PAGE 2

Date	Account Titles and Description	PR	Dr.	Cr.

SG-136

PROBLEM 5A-2 OR PROBLEM 5B-2 (CONTINUED)

CASH   ACCOUNT NO. <u>112</u>

Date	Explanation	Post Ref.	Debit	Credit	Balance Debit	Balance Credit

PREPAID INSURANCE   ACCOUNT NO. <u>114</u>

Date	Explanation	Post Ref.	Debit	Credit	Balance Debit	Balance Credit

CLEANING SUPPLIES   ACCOUNT NO. <u>115</u>

Date	Explanation	Post Ref.	Debit	Credit	Balance Debit	Balance Credit

AUTO   ACCOUNT NO. <u>121</u>

Date	Explanation	Post Ref.	Debit	Credit	Balance Debit	Balance Credit

ACCUMULATED DEPRECIATION, AUTO   ACCOUNT NO. <u>122</u>

Date	Explanation	Post Ref.	Debit	Credit	Balance Debit	Balance Credit

PROBLEM 5A-2 OR PROBLEM 5B-2 (CONTINUED)

ACCOUNTS PAYABLE — ACCOUNT NO. 212

Date	Explanation	Post Ref.	Debit	Credit	Balance Debit	Balance Credit

SALARIES PAYABLE — ACCOUNT NO. 213

Date	Explanation	Post Ref.	Debit	Credit	Balance Debit	Balance Credit

B. POTTER, CAPITAL — ACCOUNT NO. 312

Date	Explanation	Post Ref.	Debit	Credit	Balance Debit	Balance Credit

B. POTTER, WITHDRAWALS — ACCOUNT NO. 313

Date	Explanation	Post Ref.	Debit	Credit	Balance Debit	Balance Credit

INCOME SUMMARY — ACCOUNT NO. 314

Date	Explanation	Post Ref.	Debit	Credit	Balance Debit	Balance Credit

Name _____ Class _____ Date _____

PROBLEM 5A-2 OR PROBLEM 5B-2 (CONTINUED)

CLEANING FEES   **ACCOUNT NO. 412**

Date	Explanation	Post Ref.	Debit	Credit	Balance Debit	Balance Credit

SALARIES EXPENSE   **ACCOUNT NO. 513**

Date	Explanation	Post Ref.	Debit	Credit	Balance Debit	Balance Credit

TELEPHONE EXPENSE   **ACCOUNT NO. 514**

Date	Explanation	Post Ref.	Debit	Credit	Balance Debit	Balance Credit

ADVERTISING EXPENSE   **ACCOUNT NO. 515**

Date	Explanation	Post Ref.	Debit	Credit	Balance Debit	Balance Credit

GAS EXPENSE   **ACCOUNT NO. 516**

Date	Explanation	Post Ref.	Debit	Credit	Balance Debit	Balance Credit

PROBLEM 5A-2 OR PROBLEM 5B-2 (CONTINUED)

INSURANCE EXPENSE   **ACCOUNT NO. 517**

Date	Explanation	Post Ref.	Debit	Credit	Balance Debit	Balance Credit

CLEANING SUPPLIES EXPENSE   **ACCOUNT NO. 518**

Date	Explanation	Post Ref.	Debit	Credit	Balance Debit	Balance Credit

DEPRECIATION EXPENSE, AUTO   **ACCOUNT NO. 519**

Date	Explanation	Post Ref.	Debit	Credit	Balance Debit	Balance Credit

Name _____ Class _____ Date _____

PROBLEM 5A-2 OR PROBLEM 5B-2 (CONCLUDED)

(2)

POTTER CLEANING SERVICE
POST-CLOSING TRIAL BALANCE
MARCH 31, 200X

	Dr.	Cr.

PROBLEM 5A-3 OR PROBLEM 5B-3

Use one of the blank fold-out worksheets that accompanied your textbook.

PROBLEM 5A-3 OR PROBLEM 5B-3 (CONTINUED)

PETE'S PLOWING
GENERAL JOURNAL

PAGE 1

Date	Account Titles and Description	PR	Dr.	Cr.

PROBLEM 5A-3 OR PROBLEM 5B-3 (CONTINUED)

PETE'S PLOWING
GENERAL JOURNAL

PAGE 2

Date	Account Titles and Description	PR	Dr.	Cr.

PROBLEM 5A-3 OR PROBLEM 5B-3 (CONTINUED)

PETE'S PLOWING
GENERAL JOURNAL

PAGE 3

Date	Account Titles and Description	PR	Dr.	Cr.

Name _____ Class _____ Date _____

PROBLEM 5A-3 OR PROBLEM 5B-3 (CONTINUED)

CASH   ACCOUNT NO. 111

Date	Explanation	Post Ref.	Debit	Credit	Balance Debit	Balance Credit

ACCOUNTS RECEIVABLE   ACCOUNT NO. 112

Date	Explanation	Post Ref.	Debit	Credit	Balance Debit	Balance Credit

PREPAID RENT   ACCOUNT NO. 114

Date	Explanation	Post Ref.	Debit	Credit	Balance Debit	Balance Credit

SNOW SUPPLIES   ACCOUNT NO. 115

Date	Explanation	Post Ref.	Debit	Credit	Balance Debit	Balance Credit

PROBLEM 5A-3 OR PROBLEM 5B-3 (CONTINUED)

OFFICE EQUIPMENT ACCOUNT NO. 121

Date	Explanation	Post Ref.	Debit	Credit	Balance Debit	Balance Credit

ACCUMULATED DEPRECIATION, OFFICE EQUIPMENT ACCOUNT NO. 122

Date	Explanation	Post Ref.	Debit	Credit	Balance Debit	Balance Credit

SNOW EQUIPMENT ACCOUNT NO. 123

Date	Explanation	Post Ref.	Debit	Credit	Balance Debit	Balance Credit

ACCUMULATED DEPRECIATION, SNOW EQUIPMENT ACCOUNT NO. 124

Date	Explanation	Post Ref.	Debit	Credit	Balance Debit	Balance Credit

ACCOUNTS PAYABLE ACCOUNT NO. 211

Date	Explanation	Post Ref.	Debit	Credit	Balance Debit	Balance Credit

PROBLEM 5A-3 OR PROBLEM 5B-3 (CONTINUED)

SALARIES PAYABLE — ACCOUNT NO. 212

Date	Explanation	Post Ref.	Debit	Credit	Balance Debit	Balance Credit

PETE MACK, CAPITAL — ACCOUNT NO. 311

Date	Explanation	Post Ref.	Debit	Credit	Balance Debit	Balance Credit

PETE MACK, WITHDRAWALS — ACCOUNT NO. 312

Date	Explanation	Post Ref.	Debit	Credit	Balance Debit	Balance Credit

INCOME SUMMARY — ACCOUNT NO. 313

Date	Explanation	Post Ref.	Debit	Credit	Balance Debit	Balance Credit

PLOWING FEES — ACCOUNT NO. 411

Date	Explanation	Post Ref.	Debit	Credit	Balance Debit	Balance Credit

Name _____ Class _____ Date _____

PROBLEM 5A-3 OR PROBLEM 5B-3 (CONTINUED)

SALARIES EXPENSE   ACCOUNT NO. 511

Date	Explanation	Post Ref.	Debit	Credit	Balance Debit	Balance Credit

ADVERTISING EXPENSE   ACCOUNT NO. 512

Date	Explanation	Post Ref.	Debit	Credit	Balance Debit	Balance Credit

TELEPHONE EXPENSE   ACCOUNT NO. 513

Date	Explanation	Post Ref.	Debit	Credit	Balance Debit	Balance Credit

RENT EXPENSE   ACCOUNT NO. 514

Date	Explanation	Post Ref.	Debit	Credit	Balance Debit	Balance Credit

SNOW SUPPLIES EXPENSE   ACCOUNT NO. 515

Date	Explanation	Post Ref.	Debit	Credit	Balance Debit	Balance Credit

PROBLEM 5A-3 OR PROBLEM 5B-3 (CONTINUED)

DEPRECIATION EXPENSE, OFFICE EQUIPMENT   ACCOUNT NO. 516

Date	Explanation	Post Ref.	Debit	Credit	Balance Debit	Balance Credit

DEPRECIATION EXPENSE, SNOW EQUIPMENT   ACCOUNT NO. 517

Date	Explanation	Post Ref.	Debit	Credit	Balance Debit	Balance Credit

PROBLEM 5A-3 OR PROBLEM 5B-3 (CONTINUED)

PETE'S PLOWING
INCOME STATEMENT
FOR MONTH ENDED JANUARY 31, 200X

PETE'S PLOWING
STATEMENT OF OWNER'S EQUITY
FOR MONTH ENDED JANUARY 31, 200X

Name _____ Class _____ Date _____

PROBLEM 5A-3 OR PROBLEM 5B-3 (CONTINUED)

PETE'S PLOWING
BALANCE SHEET
JANUARY 31, 200X

ASSETS

LIABILITIES AND OWNER'S EQUITY

SG-151

PROBLEM 5A-3 OR PROBLEM 5B-3 (CONCLUDED)

PETE'S PLOWING
POST-CLOSING TRIAL BALANCE
JANUARY 31, 200X

		Dr.	Cr.

CHAPTER 5
SUMMARY PRACTICE TEST:
THE ACCOUNTING CYCLE COMPLETED: ADJUSTING, CLOSING, AND THE POST-CLOSING TRIAL BALANCE

Part I Instructions

Fill in the blank(s) to complete the statement.

1. After the closing process only _____ accounts remain with balances.
2. Revenue, Expenses, and Withdrawals are examples of _____ _____.
3. _____ in temporary accounts will not be carried over to the next accounting period.
4. After closing entries are posted, owner's Capital in the ledger will contain the _____ _____.
5. Revenue is closed to Income Summary by a(n) _____ to each revenue account and a(n) _____ to Income Summary.
6. Expenses are closed to Income Summary by _____ the individual expenses and _____ Income Summary.
7. If the balance of Income Summary is a credit, it will be closed by _____ Income Summary and _____ owner's Capital.
8. The balance of Withdrawals is closed by a(n) _____ and the amount transferred to owner's Capital by a(n) _____.
9. At the end of the closing process, all temporary accounts in the ledger will have a(n) _____ balance.
10. The _____ _____ _____ _____ contains a list of permanent accounts after the adjusting and closing entries have been posted to the ledger from a journal.
11. Closing entries can be prepared from a(n) _____.
12. After closing entries are posted, Income Summary will have a(n) _____ balance.
13. Journalizing adjustments can be done from the _____.
14. Cash, Equipment, and Supplies are not part of the _____ process.
15. Income Summary is a(n) _____ account.

Part II Instructions

The following is a chart of accounts for Al's Auto Shop. From the chart, indicate in Column B (by account number) which accounts will be debited or credited as related to the transactions in Column A.

Name _____ Class _____ Date _____

CHART OF ACCOUNTS

ASSETS	OWNER'S EQUITY
112 Cash	340 A. Jones, Capital
114 Accounts Receivable	341 A. Jones, Withdrawals
116 Prepaid Rent	342 Income Summary
118 Auto Supplies	
120 Delivery Truck	REVENUE
121 Accumulated Depreciation, Delivery Truck	450 Fees Earned
LIABILITIES	EXPENSES
230 Accounts Payable	560 Salaries
232 Salaries Payable	562 Advertising
	564 Rent
	566 Auto Supplies
	568 Depreciation Expense, Delivery Truck

COLUMN A	COLUMN B	
	Debit(s)	Credit(s)

1. Closed balance in revenue account to Income Summary. _____ _____
2. Closed balance in individual expenses to Income Summary. _____ _____
3. Closed balance in Income Summary to owner's Capital. (Assume that it is a net income.) _____ _____
4. Closed Withdrawals to owner's Capital. _____ _____
5. Recorded auto supplies used up. _____ _____
6. Recorded depreciation on delivery truck. _____ _____
7. Brought Salaries Expense up to date (an adjustment). _____ _____

Part III Instructions

Answer true or false to the following statements.

1. Closing entries are done every other month.
2. Adjustments are journalized before preparing the worksheet.
3. Closing entries can only clear permanent accounts.
4. Income summary is a temporary account.
5. Interim statements can be prepared from worksheets.
6. To clear expenses in the closing process, a compound entry is appropriate.
7. Withdrawals is a temporary account on the income statement.
8. Income Summary helps update withdrawals.

9. Accumulated Depreciation is a permanent account on the income statement.
10. Cash, Rent Expense, and Accounts Receivable need to be closed at the end of the period.
11. Closing entries do not relate to the worksheet.
12. Revenue is closed by a credit.
13. Expenses are placed on the debit side of the Income Summary account.
14. A post-closing trial balance closely resembles the ending balance sheet.
15. Accumulated Depreciation never has to be adjusted.
16. Interim statements are always prepared monthly.
17. A post-closing trial balance is prepared before adjustments are journalized.
18. Income Summary is shown on the balance sheet.
19. The process of closing entries will help update owner's Capital.
20. The normal balance of the Income Summary is a debit.
21. The normal balance of the Income Summary is a credit.
22. The income statement is listed in terms of debits and credits.
23. Closing updates only permanent accounts.
24. The completion of financial statements means that the Capital account in the ledger has been updated.
25. Withdrawals is closed to Income Summary.

SOLUTIONS TO SUMMARY PRACTICE TEST

Part I

1. permanent
2. temporary accounts
3. Balances
4. ending figure (balance)
5. debit, credit
6. crediting, debiting
7. debiting, crediting
8. credit, debit
9. zero
10. post-closing trial balance
11. worksheet
12. zero
13. worksheet
14. closing
15. temporary

Part II

	Debit	Credit
1.	450	342
2.	342	560, 562, 564, 566, 568
3.	342	340
4.	340	341
5.	566	118
6.	568	121
7.	560	232

Name _____ Class _____ Date _____

Part III

1. false	7. false	13. true	19. true	25. false
2. false	8. false	14. true	20. false	
3. false	9. false	15. false	21. false	
4. true	10. false	16. false	22. false	
5. true	11. false	17. false	23. false	
6. true	12. false	18. false	24. false	

CONTINUING PROBLEM FOR CHAPTER 5

SANCHEZ COMPUTER CENTER
GENERAL JOURNAL

PAGE 2

Date	Account Titles and Description	PR	Dr.	Cr.

Name _____ Class _____ Date _____

CASH   ACCOUNT NO. 1000

Date	Explanation	Post Ref.	Debit	Credit	Balance Debit	Balance Credit
9/30 0X	Balance forward	✔			1,645.00	

ACCOUNTS RECEIVABLE   ACCOUNT NO. 1020

Date	Explanation	Post Ref.	Debit	Credit	Balance Debit	Balance Credit
9/30 0X	Balance forward	✔			2,600.00	

PREPAID RENT   ACCOUNT NO. 1025

Date	Explanation	Post Ref.	Debit	Credit	Balance Debit	Balance Credit
9/30 0X	Balance forward	✔			1,200.00	

SUPPLIES   ACCOUNT NO. 1030

Date	Explanation	Post Ref.	Debit	Credit	Balance Debit	Balance Credit
9/30 0X	Balance forward	✔			450.00	

COMPUTER SHOP EQUIPMENT   ACCOUNT NO. 1080

Date		Explanation	Post Ref.	Debit	Credit	Balance Debit	Balance Credit
9/30	0X	Balance forward	✔			2 4 0 0 00	

ACCUMULATED DEPRECIATION, COMPUTER SHOP EQUIPMENT   ACCOUNT NO. 1081

Date	Explanation	Post Ref.	Debit	Credit	Balance Debit	Balance Credit

OFFICE EQUIPMENT   ACCOUNT NO. 1090

Date		Explanation	Post Ref.	Debit	Credit	Balance Debit	Balance Credit
9/30	0X	Balance forward	✔			6 0 0 00	

ACCUMULATED DEPRECIATION, OFFICE EQUIPMENT   ACCOUNT NO. 1091

Date	Explanation	Post Ref.	Debit	Credit	Balance Debit	Balance Credit

Name _____ Class _____ Date _____

ACCOUNTS PAYABLE   ACCOUNT NO. <u>2000</u>

Date	Explanation	Post Ref.	Debit	Credit	Balance Debit	Balance Credit
9/30 0X	Balance forward	✓				2 1 0 00

T. FREEDMAN, CAPITAL   ACCOUNT NO. <u>3000</u>

Date	Explanation	Post Ref.	Debit	Credit	Balance Debit	Balance Credit
9/30 0X	Balance forward	✓				4 5 0 0 00

T. FREEDMAN, WITHDRAWALS   ACCOUNT NO. <u>3010</u>

Date	Explanation	Post Ref.	Debit	Credit	Balance Debit	Balance Credit
9/30 0X	Balance forward	✓			1 0 0 00	

INCOME SUMMARY   ACCOUNT NO. 3020

Date	Explanation	Post Ref.	Debit	Credit	Balance Debit	Balance Credit

SERVICE REVENUE   ACCOUNT NO. 4000

Date	Explanation	Post Ref.	Debit	Credit	Balance Debit	Balance Credit
9/30 0X	Balance forward	✓				6 685 00

ADVERTISING EXPENSE   ACCOUNT NO. 5010

Date	Explanation	Post Ref.	Debit	Credit	Balance Debit	Balance Credit
9/30 0X	Balance forward	✓			1 400 00	

RENT EXPENSE   ACCOUNT NO. 5020

Date	Explanation	Post Ref.	Debit	Credit	Balance Debit	Balance Credit
9/30 0X	Balance forward	✓			400 00	

Name _____ Class _____ Date _____

UTILITIES EXPENSE   ACCOUNT NO. 5030

Date	Explanation	Post Ref.	Debit	Credit	Balance Debit	Balance Credit
9/30 0X	Balance forward	✔			180 00	

PHONE EXPENSE   ACCOUNT NO. 5040

Date	Explanation	Post Ref.	Debit	Credit	Balance Debit	Balance Credit
9/30 0X	Balance forward	✔			220 00	

SUPPLIES EXPENSE   ACCOUNT NO. 5050

Date	Explanation	Post Ref.	Debit	Credit	Balance Debit	Balance Credit

INSURANCE EXPENSE   ACCOUNT NO. 5060

Date	Explanation	Post Ref.	Debit	Credit	Balance Debit	Balance Credit
9/30 0X	Balance forward	✔			150 00	

Name _____ Class _____ Date _____

POSTAGE EXPENSE   ACCOUNT NO. 5070

Date		Explanation	Post Ref.	Debit	Credit	Balance Debit	Balance Credit
9/30	0X	Balance forward	✔			5 0 00	

DEPRECIATION EXPENSE C.S. EQUIPMENT   ACCOUNT NO. 5080

Date	Explanation	Post Ref.	Debit	Credit	Balance Debit	Balance Credit

DEPRECIATION EXPENSE OFFICE EQUIPMENT   ACCOUNT NO. 5090

Date	Explanation	Post Ref.	Debit	Credit	Balance Debit	Balance Credit

SANCHEZ COMPUTER CENTER
POST-CLOSING TRIAL BALANCE
SEPTEMBER 30, 200X

		Dr.	Cr.

MINI PRACTICE SET
SULLIVAN REALTY

SULLIVAN REALTY
GENERAL JOURNAL

PAGE 1

Date	Account Titles and Description	PR	Dr.	Cr.

Name _____ Class _____ Date _____

MINI PRACTICE SET
SULLIVAN REALTY

SULLIVAN REALTY
GENERAL JOURNAL

PAGE 2

Date	Account Titles and Description	PR	Dr.	Cr.

MINI PRACTICE SET
SULLIVAN REALTY

SULLIVAN REALTY
GENERAL JOURNAL

PAGE 3

Date	Account Titles and Description	PR	Dr.	Cr.

MINI PRACTICE SET
SULLIVAN REALTY

SULLIVAN REALTY
GENERAL JOURNAL

PAGE 4

Date	Account Titles and Description	PR	Dr.	Cr.

MINI PRACTICE SET
SULLIVAN REALTY

SULLIVAN REALTY
GENERAL JOURNAL

PAGE 5

Date	Account Titles and Description	PR	Dr.	Cr.

MINI PRACTICE SET
SULLIVAN REALTY

SULLIVAN REALTY
GENERAL JOURNAL

PAGE 6

Date	Account Titles and Description	PR	Dr.	Cr.

MINI PRACTICE SET
SULLIVAN REALTY

CASH   **ACCOUNT NO. 111**

Date	Explanation	Post Ref.	Debit	Credit	Balance Debit	Balance Credit

MINI PRACTICE SET
SULLIVAN REALTY

ACCOUNTS RECEIVABLE   ACCOUNT NO. 112

Date	Explanation	Post Ref.	Debit	Credit	Balance Debit	Balance Credit

PREPAID RENT   ACCOUNT NO. 114

Date	Explanation	Post Ref.	Debit	Credit	Balance Debit	Balance Credit

OFFICE SUPPLIES   ACCOUNT NO. 115

Date	Explanation	Post Ref.	Debit	Credit	Balance Debit	Balance Credit

OFFICE EQUIPMENT   ACCOUNT NO. 121

Date	Explanation	Post Ref.	Debit	Credit	Balance Debit	Balance Credit

MINI PRACTICE SET: SULLIVAN REALTY

ACCUMULATED DEPRECIATION, OFFICE EQUIPMENT   ACCOUNT NO. 122

Date	Explanation	Post Ref.	Debit	Credit	Balance Debit	Balance Credit

AUTOMOBILE   ACCOUNT NO. 123

Date	Explanation	Post Ref.	Debit	Credit	Balance Debit	Balance Credit

ACCUMULATED DEPRECIATION, AUTOMOBILE   ACCOUNT NO. 124

Date	Explanation	Post Ref.	Debit	Credit	Balance Debit	Balance Credit

ACCOUNTS PAYABLE   ACCOUNT NO. 211

Date	Explanation	Post Ref.	Debit	Credit	Balance Debit	Balance Credit

SALARIES PAYABLE   ACCOUNT NO. 212

Date	Explanation	Post Ref.	Debit	Credit	Balance Debit	Balance Credit

Name _____ Class _____ Date _____

MINI PRACTICE SET
SULLIVAN REALTY

JOHN SULLIVAN, CAPITAL   ACCOUNT NO. 311

Date	Explanation	Post Ref.	Debit	Credit	Balance Debit	Balance Credit

JOHN SULLIVAN, WITHDRAWALS   ACCOUNT NO. 312

Date	Explanation	Post Ref.	Debit	Credit	Balance Debit	Balance Credit

INCOME SUMMARY   ACCOUNT NO. 313

Date	Explanation	Post Ref.	Debit	Credit	Balance Debit	Balance Credit

Name _____ Class _____ Date _____

MINI PRACTICE SET
SULLIVAN REALTY

COMMISSIONS EARNED   **ACCOUNT NO. 411**

Date	Explanation	Post Ref.	Debit	Credit	Balance Debit	Balance Credit

RENT EXPENSE   **ACCOUNT NO. 511**

Date	Explanation	Post Ref.	Debit	Credit	Balance Debit	Balance Credit

SALARIES EXPENSE   **ACCOUNT NO. 512**

Date	Explanation	Post Ref.	Debit	Credit	Balance Debit	Balance Credit

Name _____ Class _____ Date _____

MINI PRACTICE SET
SULLIVAN REALTY

GAS EXPENSE   **ACCOUNT NO. 513**

Date	Explanation	Post Ref.	Debit	Credit	Balance Debit	Balance Credit

REPAIRS EXPENSE   **ACCOUNT NO. 514**

Date	Explanation	Post Ref.	Debit	Credit	Balance Debit	Balance Credit

TELEPHONE EXPENSE   **ACCOUNT NO. 515**

Date	Explanation	Post Ref.	Debit	Credit	Balance Debit	Balance Credit

ADVERTISING EXPENSE   **ACCOUNT NO. 516**

Date	Explanation	Post Ref.	Debit	Credit	Balance Debit	Balance Credit

Name _____ Class _____ Date _____

MINI PRACTICE SET
SULLIVAN REALTY

OFFICE SUPPLIES EXPENSE ACCOUNT NO. **517**

Date	Explanation	Post Ref.	Debit	Credit	Balance Debit	Balance Credit

DEPRECIATION EXPENSE, OFFICE EQUIPMENT ACCOUNT NO. **518**

Date	Explanation	Post Ref.	Debit	Credit	Balance Debit	Balance Credit

DEPRECIATION EXPENSE, AUTOMOBILE ACCOUNT NO. **519**

Date	Explanation	Post Ref.	Debit	Credit	Balance Debit	Balance Credit

MISCELLANEOUS EXPENSE ACCOUNT NO. **524**

Date	Explanation	Post Ref.	Debit	Credit	Balance Debit	Balance Credit

MINI PRACTICE SET
SULLIVAN REALTY

Use the blank fold-out worksheets that accompanied your textbook.

SULLIVAN REALTY
INCOME STATEMENT
FOR MONTH ENDED JUNE 30, 200X

MINI PRACTICE SET
SULLIVAN REALTY

SULLIVAN REALTY
STATEMENT OF OWNER'S EQUITY
FOR MONTH ENDED JUNE 30, 200X

Name _____ Class _____ Date _____

**MINI PRACTICE SET
SULLIVAN REALTY**

SG-180

Name _____ Class _____ Date _____

MINI PRACTICE SET
SULLIVAN REALTY

SULLIVAN REALTY
POST-CLOSING TRIAL BALANCE
JUNE 30, 200X

		Dr.	Cr.

You can find the worksheet for July with the blank fold-out worksheets that accompanied your textbook.

SG-181

Name _____ Class _____ Date _____

MINI PRACTICE SET
SULLIVAN REALTY

SULLIVAN REALTY
INCOME STATEMENT
FOR MONTH ENDED JULY 31, 200X

**MINI PRACTICE SET
SULLIVAN REALTY**

**SULLIVAN REALTY
STATEMENT OF OWNER'S EQUITY
FOR MONTH ENDED JULY 31, 200X**

**MINI PRACTICE SET
SULLIVAN REALTY**

Name_____ Class_____ Date_____

MINI PRACTICE SET
SULLIVAN REALTY

SULLIVAN REALTY
POST-CLOSING TRIAL BALANCE
JULY 31, 200X

		Dr.	Cr.

Banking Procedures and Control of Cash

SELF-REVIEW QUIZ 6-1

Situation	Add to Bank Balance	Deduct from Bank Balance	Add to Checkbook Balance	Deduct from Checkbook Balance
1				
2				
3				
4				
5				
6				
7				
8				

SELF-REVIEW QUIZ 6-2

PAGE 6

Date	Account Titles and Description	PR	Dr.	Cr.

AUXILIARY PETTY CASH RECORD

Date	Voucher No.	Description	Receipts	Payment	Category of Payment					
					Delivery Expense	General Expense	Account	Sundry Amount	

Name _____ Class _____ Date _____

CHAPTER 6
SET A   **FORMS FOR CLASSROOM DEMONSTRATION EXERCISES**

1.
- A. _____
- B. _____
- C. _____
- D. _____
- E. _____
- F. _____

2. _____ _____ _____ _____

3.

ACE CO.
BANK RECONCILIATION
JUNE 30, 200X

Checkbook	Bank

4.
- A. _____ _____ _____
- B. _____ _____ _____
- C. _____ _____ _____
- D. _____ _____ _____
- E. _____ _____ _____
- F. _____ _____ _____

5.

6.

SG-188

Name _____ Class _____ Date _____

SET B

CHAPTER 6
FORMS FOR CLASSROOM DEMONSTRATION EXERCISES

1.
- A. _____
- B. _____
- C. _____
- D. _____
- E. _____
- F. _____

2. _____ _____ _____ _____

3.

ACE CO.
BANK RECONCILIATION
JUNE 30, 200X

Checkbook	Bank

4.
- A. _____ _____ _____
- B. _____ _____ _____
- C. _____ _____ _____
- D. _____ _____ _____
- E. _____ _____ _____
- F. _____ _____ _____

5.

6.

SG-189

FORMS FOR EXERCISES

6-1.

BING CO.
BANK RECONCILIATION AS OF JULY 31, 200X

CHECKBOOK BALANCE		BALANCE PER BANK	
Ending Checkbook Balance	_____	Ending Bank Statement Balance	_____
Deduct:		Add:	
Bank Service Charge	_____	Deposit in Transit	_____
	_____		_____
	_____	Deduct:	
	_____	Outstanding Checks	_____
	_____		_____
Reconciled Balance	_____	Reconciled Balance	_____

6-2.

6-3.

EXERCISES (CONCLUDED)

6-4.

6-5.

    Beg. Change Fund
+Cash Register Total
=Cash should have on hand
− Counted Cash
= Cash Shortage

Name _____ Class _____ Date _____

END OF CHAPTER PROBLEMS

PROBLEM 6A-1 OR PROBLEM 6B-1

LEE.COM
BANK RECONCILIATION AS OF JULY 31, 200X

BALANCE PER BANK		CHECKBOOK BALANCE	
Bank Statement Balance		Checkbook Balance	
Add:	_____	Add:	
Deduct:	_____		_____
	_____	Deduct:	
			_____
Reconciled Balance	_____	Reconciled Balance	_____

PROBLEM 6A-1 OR PROBLEM 6B-1 (CONCLUDED)

Date	Account Titles and Description	PR	Dr.	Cr.

Name _____ Class _____ Date _____

PROBLEM 6A-2 OR PROBLEM 6B-2

LOWELL NATIONAL BANK
RIO MEAN BRAND
BUGNA, TEXAS   TELEPHONE 555-8311

This form is provided to help you balance your bank statement. If no errors are reported to auditors in ten days, the account will be considered correct.

Please notify us of any change in address.

Checks outstanding
(not charged to account)

Check No.	Amount
Total	

Sort the checks numerically or by date issued.
Check off on the stubs of your checkbook each check paid by bank.
List the numbers and amounts of checks still outstanding in the space provided at the left.
Verify the deposits in your checkbook with deposits credited on this statement. Bank balance show on this statement $_____
Plus: Deposits not
   credited on this statement $_____
      Subtotal $_____
Less: Checks outstanding $_____
Balance $_____

If your checkbook does not agree, enter any necessary adjustments:
_____
_____
_____

Correct checkbook balance $_____

SG-194

Name _____ Class _____ Date _____

PROBLEM 6A-2 OR PROBLEM 6B-2 (CONCLUDED)

GENERAL JOURNAL

Date	Account Titles and Description	PR	Dr.	Cr.

SG-195

PROBLEM 6A-3 OR PROBLEM 6B-3

MERRY CO.
GENERAL JOURNAL

Date	Account Titles and Description	PR	Dr.	Cr.

PROBLEM 6A-3 OR PROBLEM 6B-3 (CONCLUDED)

MERRY CO.
AUXILIARY PETTY CASH RECORD

| Date | Voucher No. | Description | Receipts | Payment | Category of Payment |||||
					Postage Expense	Office Supplies Expense	Account	Sundry Amount

PROBLEM 6A-4 OR PROBLEM 6B-4

LOGAN CO.
GENERAL JOURNAL

PAGE 2

Date	Account Titles and Description	PR	Dr.	Cr.

PROBLEM 6A-4 OR PROBLEM 6B-4 (CONCLUDED)

LOGAN CO.
AUXILIARY PETTY CASH RECORD

Date	Voucher No.	Description	Receipts	Payment	Category of Payment			
					Postage Expense	Delivery Expense	Sundry		
							Account	Amount

SG-199

Name _____ Class _____ Date _____

CHAPTER 6
SUMMARY PRACTICE TEST
BANKING PROCEDURES AND CONTROL OF CASH

Part I Instructions

Fill in the blank(s) to complete the statement.

1. Online banking is _____ due to the internet.
2. Today, use of the _____ _____ has greatly increased.
3. All adjustments to the checkbook balance in the reconciliation process will require _____ _____.
4. Petty cash is a(n) _____ found on the balance sheet.
5. The auxiliary petty cash record is not a(n) _____.
6. A(n) _____ _____ is an asset used to make change for customer.
7. A cash overage will be _____ _____ on the income statement.
8. _____ _____ represents checks not processed by the bank at the time the bank statement was prepared.
9. When a bank credits your account, your balance will _____.
10. _____ is a procedure whereby the bank does not return the processed checks.

Part II Instructions

Indicate which of the following procedures are involved in each of the transactions below.

a. Recorded in General Journal
b. Recorded in both general journal and auxiliary petty cash record
c. Recorded only in auxiliary petty cash record
d. New check is written
e. Account petty cash is increased

1. EXAMPLE: Check issued to establish petty cash   b,d,e
2. Paid donation from petty cash   _____
3. Paid postage from petty cash   _____
4. Paid past purchases previously charged   _____
5. Paid for business luncheon with petty cash   _____
6. Issued check to pay for office supplies   _____
7. Replenished petty cash   _____
8. Paid local donation from petty cash   _____
9. Paid for past purchases bought on account   _____
10. Replenished petty cash   _____

Name _____ Class _____ Date _____

Part III Instructions

Answer true or false to the following statements.

1. Online banking is decreasing today.
2. Petty cash is a liability found on the balance sheet.
3. Checks returned from the bank are placed in alphabetical order.
4. ATMs are being used less today than in the past.
5. Bank service charges represent an expense to the business.
6. The bank statement is the same as the bank reconciliation.
7. The balance in the company cash account will always equal the bank balance before the bank statement is received.
8. Deposit slips are needed in writing checks.
9. The signature must be presented when cashing a check.
10. The auxiliary petty cash record is posted monthly.
11. The petty cash account has a debit balance.
12. Replenishment of petty cash requires a new check.
13. The expenses paid from petty cash are journalized at time of replenishment.
14. Internal control only affects large companies.
15. A petty cash voucher records the expense into the ledger.
16. The petty cash fund must be replenished monthly.
17. The petty cash voucher identifies the account that will be charged.
18. The establishment of petty cash may require some judgment as to the amount of petty cash needed.
19. EFT is the same as safekeeping.
20. The drawer is the person who receives the check.
21. A debit memo will increase the depositor's balance.
22. A change fund uses only one denomination.
23. The payer is the person or company the check is payable to.

Part IV Instructions

Based on the following situation, prepare a bank reconciliation.

The checkbook balance of Logan Company is $5,263.08. The bank statement shows a bank balance of $7,980. The bank statement shows interest earned of $42 and a service charge of $29.76. There is a deposit in transit of $2,558.22. Outstanding checks total $3,762.90. The bank collected a note for Moore for $4,200. Moore Company forgot to deduct a check for $2,700 during the month.

SOLUTIONS TO SUMMARY PRACTICE TEST

Part I

1. increasing
2. debit card
3. journal entries
4. asset
5. journal
6. change fund
7. miscellaneous income
8. Checks outstanding
9. increase
10. Safekeeping

Part II

1. b, d, e
2. c
3. c
4. a, d
5. c
6. a, d
7. b, d
8. c
9. a, d
10. b, d

Part III

1. false
2. false
3. false
4. false
5. true
6. false
7. false
8. false
9. true
10. false
11. true
12. true
13. true
14. false
15. false
16. false
17. true
18. true
19. false
20. false
21. false
22. false
23. false

Part IV

LOGAN CO.			BANK BALANCE	
Checkbook Balance		$5,263.08	Bank Balance	$7,980.00
ADD:			ADD:	
			Deposit	
Interest	$ 42		in Transit	2,558.22
Collection of note	4,200	4,242.00		$9,038.22
		8,005.08		
DEDUCT:			DEDUCT:	
Service Chg.	$ 29.76		Check outstanding	$3,762.90
Error	2,700.00	2,729.76		
Reconciled Balance		$6,775.32	Reconciled Balance	$6,775.32

SG-202

CONTINUING PROBLEM FOR CHAPTER 6

SANCHEZ COMPUTER CENTER
GENERAL JOURNAL

PAGE 3

Date	Account Titles and Description	PR	Dr.	Cr.

Name _____ Class _____ Date _____

CASH   **ACCOUNT NO. 1000**

Date		Explanation	Post Ref.	Debit	Credit	Balance Debit	Balance Credit
9/30	0X	Balance forward	✔			1 6 4 5 00	

PETTY CASH   **ACCOUNT NO. 1010**

Date		Explanation	Post Ref.	Debit	Credit	Balance Debit	Balance Credit

ACCOUNTS RECEIVABLE   ACCOUNT NO. 1020

Date		Explanation	Post Ref.	Debit	Credit	Balance Debit	Balance Credit
9/30	0X	Balance forward	✔			2,600.00	

PREPAID RENT   ACCOUNT NO. 1025

Date		Explanation	Post Ref.	Debit	Credit	Balance Debit	Balance Credit
9/30	0X	Balance forward	✔			400.00	

SUPPLIES   ACCOUNT NO. 1030

Date		Explanation	Post Ref.	Debit	Credit	Balance Debit	Balance Credit
9/30	0X	Balance forward	✔			90.00	

COMPUTER SHOP EQUIPMENT   ACCOUNT NO. 1080

Date		Explanation	Post Ref.	Debit	Credit	Balance Debit	Balance Credit
9/30	0X	Balance forward	✔			2,400.00	

ACCUMULATED DEPRECIATION, COMPUTER SHOP EQUIPMENT — ACCOUNT NO. 1081

Date		Explanation	Post Ref.	Debit	Credit	Balance Debit	Balance Credit
9/30	0X	Balance forward	✔				99 00

OFFICE EQUIPMENT — ACCOUNT NO. 1090

Date		Explanation	Post Ref.	Debit	Credit	Balance Debit	Balance Credit
9/30	0X	Balance forward	✔			600 00	

ACCUMULATED DEPRECIATION, OFFICE EQUIPMENT — ACCOUNT NO. 1091

Date		Explanation	Post Ref.	Debit	Credit	Balance Debit	Balance Credit
9/30	0X	Balance forward	✔				20 00

ACCOUNTS PAYABLE — ACCOUNT NO. 2000

Date		Explanation	Post Ref.	Debit	Credit	Balance Debit	Balance Credit
9/30	0X	Balance forward	✔				210 00

Name _____ Class _____ Date _____

T. FREEDMAN, CAPITAL   ACCOUNT NO. **3000**

Date		Explanation	Post Ref.	Debit	Credit	Balance Debit	Balance Credit
9/30	0X	Balance forward	✔				7 4 0 6 00

T. FREEDMAN, WITHDRAWALS   ACCOUNT NO. **3010**

Date	Explanation	Post Ref.	Debit	Credit	Balance Debit	Balance Credit

INCOME SUMMARY   ACCOUNT NO. **3020**

Date	Explanation	Post Ref.	Debit	Credit	Balance Debit	Balance Credit

Name _____ Class _____ Date _____

SERVICE REVENUE ACCOUNT NO. <u>4000</u>

Date	Explanation	Post Ref.	Debit	Credit	Balance Debit	Balance Credit

ADVERTISING EXPENSE ACCOUNT NO. <u>5010</u>

Date	Explanation	Post Ref.	Debit	Credit	Balance Debit	Balance Credit

RENT EXPENSE ACCOUNT NO. <u>5020</u>

Date	Explanation	Post Ref.	Debit	Credit	Balance Debit	Balance Credit

Name _____ Class _____ Date _____

UTILITIES EXPENSE ACCOUNT NO. 5030

Date	Explanation	Post Ref.	Debit	Credit	Balance Debit	Balance Credit

PHONE EXPENSE ACCOUNT NO. 5040

Date	Explanation	Post Ref.	Debit	Credit	Balance Debit	Balance Credit

SUPPLIES EXPENSE ACCOUNT NO. 5050

Date	Explanation	Post Ref.	Debit	Credit	Balance Debit	Balance Credit

INSURANCE EXPENSE ACCOUNT NO. 5060

Date	Explanation	Post Ref.	Debit	Credit	Balance Debit	Balance Credit

Name _____ Class _____ Date _____

POSTAGE EXPENSE ACCOUNT NO. **5070**

Date	Explanation	Post Ref.	Debit	Credit	Balance Debit	Balance Credit

DEPRECIATION EXPENSE, COMPUTER SHOP EQUIPMENT ACCOUNT NO. **5080**

Date	Explanation	Post Ref.	Debit	Credit	Balance Debit	Balance Credit

DEPRECIATION EXPENSE, OFFICE EQUIPMENT ACCOUNT NO. **5090**

Date	Explanation	Post Ref.	Debit	Credit	Balance Debit	Balance Credit

MISCELLANEOUS EXPENSE ACCOUNT NO. **5100**

Date	Explanation	Post Ref.	Debit	Credit	Balance Debit	Balance Credit

SANCHEZ COMPUTER CENTER
TRIAL BALANCE
OCTOBER 31, 200X

AUXILIARY PETTY CASH RECORD

Date	Voucher No.	Description	Receipts	Payment	Category of Payment			
					Postage Expense	Supplies Expense	Account	Sundry Amount

Name _____ Class _____ Date _____

SANCHEZ COMPUTER CENTER
BANK RECONCILIATION AS OF SEPTEMBER 30, 200X

BALANCE PER BANK   **CHECKBOOK BALANCE**

Bank Statement Balance   Checkbook Balance

  Add: _____   Add:

  Deduct: _____   _____
                         _____   Deduct:

                                                                                                    _____

Reconciled Balance   =============   Reconciled Balance   =============

Payroll Concepts and Procedures— Employee Taxes

7

SELF-REVIEW QUIZ 7-1

REGULAR EARNINGS _____
OVERTIME _____
GROSS EARNINGS _____

SELF-REVIEW QUIZ 7-2

FIT _____
SIT _____
FICA - OASDI _____
FICA - Medicare _____
NET PAY _____

Name _____ Class _____ Date _____

SELF-REVIEW QUIZ 7-3

FICA - OASDI _____

FICA - Medicare _____

FUTA _____

SUTA _____

Name _____ Class _____ Date _____

CHAPTER 7
SET A   **FORMS FOR CLASSROOM DEMONSTRATION EXERCISES**

1. A. _____
   _____
   _____

   B. _____
   _____
   _____

2. _____
   _____
   _____
   _____
   _____

3. _____
   _____
   _____
   _____
   _____
   _____
   _____

4. A. _____   D. _____
   B. _____   E. _____
   C. _____   F. _____

5. A. _____
   B. _____
   C. _____
   D. _____

SG-216

Name _____ Class _____ Date _____

CHAPTER 7
SET B   FORMS FOR CLASSROOM DEMONSTRATION EXERCISES

1.   A. _____

       B. _____

2. _____

3. _____

4.   A. _____   D. _____
        B. _____   E. _____
        C. _____   F. _____

5.
       A. _____
       B. _____
       C. _____
       D. _____

Name _____ Class _____ Date _____

FORMS FOR EXERCISES

7-1.

Carmen _____

Jill _____
_____

Fred _____
_____

7-2.

Alvin	Angelina
_____	_____
_____	_____
_____	_____
_____	_____
_____	_____
_____	_____
_____	_____
_____	_____

7-3. _____
_____
_____
_____
_____
_____

7-4. _____
_____
_____
_____
_____
_____

SG-218

Name _____ Class _____ Date _____

EXERCISES (CONCLUDED)

7-5. _____
_____
_____
_____
_____

7-6. _____
_____
_____
_____
_____
_____

7-7.

Employee	Weekly Pay	Weeks	Total	Taxable	Tax Rate	Tax

7-8. _____
_____
_____

Name _____ Class _____ Date _____

END OF CHAPTER PROBLEMS

PROBLEM 7A-1 OR PROBLEM 7B-1

Employee	Hourly Rate	# of Hours Worked	Gross Earnings
A.			
B.			
C.			
D.			

A.   B.

C.   D.

PROBLEM 7A-2 OR PROBLEM 7B-2

Use the fold-out payroll register that accompanied your textbook.

PROBLEM 7A-3 OR PROBLEM 7B-3

Use the fold-out payroll register that accompanied your textbook.

PROBLEM 7A-4 OR PROBLEM 7B-4

Use the fold-out payroll register that accompanied your textbook.

Name _____ Class _____ Date _____

CHAPTER 7
SUMMARY PRACTICE TEST:
PAYROLL CONCEPTS AND PROCEDURES—EMPLOYEE TAXES

PART I INSTRUCTIONS

Fill in the blank(s) to complete the statement.

1. _____ _____ is gross pay less deductions.
2. Form _____ aids the employer in knowing how much to deduct for federal income tax.
3. The base for OASDI-Medicare will _____ _____ from year to year.
4. _____ _____ of the employer's tax guide has tables available for deductions for FIT and FICA (OASDI and Medicare).
5. _____ _____ _____ protects employees against losses due to injury or death incurred while on the job.
6. The two primary records used to keep track of payroll information are the _____ _____ and _____ _____ _____.
7. The employer is responsible for paying for _____.
8. _____ _____ is paid every two weeks.
9. A(n) _____ employee will only be paid for the hours actually worked.
10. An employer must pay FUTA on wages earned by each employee up to a maximum of $_____.

Part II Instructions

Answer true or false to the following.

1. OASDI is the tax form for SUTA.
2. Employers only pay FUTA and SUTA.
3. Employers pay a higher FICA-OASDI tax rate than employees do.
4. Gross pay plus deductions equals net pay.
5. Form W-4 aids in calculating FICA-OASDI.
6. The employer will match the employee's contribution for FICA (OASDI and Medicare).
7. The maximum tax credit for state unemployment tax is .8%.
8. A company may have different types of employees.
9. The Wage-Bracket Table makes it more difficult to calculate the amount of deductions for FIT.
10. A calendar year has no effect on taxes for FICA-Social Security.

Name _____ Class _____ Date _____

Part III Instructions

Complete the chart below (use table in text as needed). Use the following information: Before this payroll Pete Bloom had earned $101,000. This week Pete earned $2,000 for the past two weeks. Assume an OASDI rate of Social Security of 6.2% up to $102,000. Medicare, 1.45%. FIT is $238.50. The state income tax is 7 percent.

GROSS PAY	TAXABLE FICA	DEDUCTIONS FICA		FIT	SIT	NET PAY
		OASDI	Med.			

CHAPTER 7
SOLUTIONS TO SUMMARY PRACTICE TEST

Part I

1. Net Pay
2. W-4
3. not change
4. Circular E
5. Workers' Compensation Insurance
6. payroll register, employee earnings record
7. FUTA (SUTA)
8. Biweekly payroll
9. hourly
10. 7,000

Part II

1. false
2. false
3. false
4. false
5. false
6. true
7. false
8. true
9. false
10. false

Part III

OASDI	$1,000 × .062 =	$ 62.00	
Medicare	2,000 × .0145 =	29.00	
FIT		238.50	$2,000.00
SIT	2,000 × .07	140.00	− 469.50
Total deductions		$469.50	$1,530.50

SG-222

CONTINUING PROBLEM FOR CHAPTER 7

(1)

SANCHEZ COMPUTER CENTER
GENERAL JOURNAL

PAGE 4

Date	Account Titles and Description	PR	Dr.	Cr.

SANCHEZ COMPUTER CENTER
GENERAL JOURNAL

PAGE 5

Date	Account Titles and Description	PR	Dr.	Cr.

Name _____ Class _____ Date _____

CASH ACCOUNT NO. 1000

Date	Explanation	Post Ref.	Debit	Credit	Balance Debit	Balance Credit
10/31 0X	Balance forward	✔			4 293 00	

PETTY CASH ACCOUNT NO. 1010

Date	Explanation	Post Ref.	Debit	Credit	Balance Debit	Balance Credit
10/31 0X	Balance forward	✔			100 00	

ACCOUNTS RECEIVABLE ACCOUNT NO. 1020

Date	Explanation	Post Ref.	Debit	Credit	Balance Debit	Balance Credit
10/31 0X	Balance forward	✔			4 200 00	

PREPAID RENT   ACCOUNT NO. <u>1025</u>

Date	Explanation	Post Ref.	Debit	Credit	Balance Debit	Balance Credit
10/31 0X	Balance forward	✓			1 600 00	

SUPPLIES   ACCOUNT NO. <u>1030</u>

Date	Explanation	Post Ref.	Debit	Credit	Balance Debit	Balance Credit
10/31 0X	Balance forward	✓			90 00	

COMPUTER SHOP EQUIPMENT   ACCOUNT NO. <u>1080</u>

Date	Explanation	Post Ref.	Debit	Credit	Balance Debit	Balance Credit
10/31 0X	Balance forward	✓			2 400 00	

ACCUMULATED DEPRECIATION, COMPUTER SHOP EQUIPMENT   ACCOUNT NO. <u>1081</u>

Date	Explanation	Post Ref.	Debit	Credit	Balance Debit	Balance Credit
10/31 0X	Balance forward	✓				99 00

OFFICE EQUIPMENT   ACCOUNT NO. 1090

Date		Explanation	Post Ref.	Debit	Credit	Balance Debit	Balance Credit
10/31	0X	Balance forward	✓			600 00	

ACCUMULATED DEPRECIATION, OFFICE EQUIPMENT   ACCOUNT NO. 1091

Date		Explanation	Post Ref.	Debit	Credit	Balance Debit	Balance Credit
10/31	0X	Balance forward	✓				20 00

ACCOUNTS PAYABLE   ACCOUNT NO. 2000

Date		Explanation	Post Ref.	Debit	Credit	Balance Debit	Balance Credit
10/31	0X	Balance forward	✓				50 00

WAGES PAYABLE   ACCOUNT NO. 2010

Date		Explanation	Post Ref.	Debit	Credit	Balance Debit	Balance Credit

Name _____ Class _____ Date _____

FICA—OASDI PAYABLE ACCOUNT NO. <u>2020</u>

Date	Explanation	Post Ref.	Debit	Credit	Balance	
					Debit	Credit

FICA—MEDICARE PAYABLE ACCOUNT NO. <u>2030</u>

Date	Explanation	Post Ref.	Debit	Credit	Balance	
					Debit	Credit

FIT PAYABLE ACCOUNT NO. <u>2040</u>

Date	Explanation	Post Ref.	Debit	Credit	Balance	
					Debit	Credit

SIT PAYABLE ACCOUNT NO. <u>2050</u>

Date	Explanation	Post Ref.	Debit	Credit	Balance	
					Debit	Credit

Name _____ Class _____ Date _____

T. FREEDMAN CAPITAL   ACCOUNT NO. 3000

Date	Explanation	Post Ref.	Debit	Credit	Balance Debit	Balance Credit
10/31 0X	Balance forward	✓				7 406 00

T. FREEDMAN WITHDRAWALS   ACCOUNT NO. 3010

Date	Explanation	Post Ref.	Debit	Credit	Balance Debit	Balance Credit
10/31 0X	Balance forward	✓			2 015 00	

SERVICE REVENUE   ACCOUNT NO. 4000

Date	Explanation	Post Ref.	Debit	Credit	Balance Debit	Balance Credit
10/31 0X	Balance forward	✓				7 800 00

ADVERTISING EXPENSE   ACCOUNT NO. 5010

Date	Explanation	Post Ref.	Debit	Credit	Balance Debit	Balance Credit

RENT EXPENSE   ACCOUNT NO. 5020

Date	Explanation	Post Ref.	Debit	Credit	Balance Debit	Balance Credit

UTILITIES EXPENSE   ACCOUNT NO. 5030

Date	Explanation	Post Ref.	Debit	Credit	Balance Debit	Balance Credit

PHONE EXPENSE   ACCOUNT NO. 5040

Date	Explanation	Post Ref.	Debit	Credit	Balance Debit	Balance Credit

SUPPLIES EXPENSE   ACCOUNT NO. 5050

Date	Explanation	Post Ref.	Debit	Credit	Balance Debit	Balance Credit
10/31 0X		✓			4 2 00	

INSURANCE EXPENSE   ACCOUNT NO. 5060

Date	Explanation	Post Ref.	Debit	Credit	Balance Debit	Balance Credit

POSTAGE EXPENSE   ACCOUNT NO. 5070

Date	Explanation	Post Ref.	Debit	Credit	Balance Debit	Balance Credit
10/31 0X	Balance forward	✓			2 5 00	

DEPRECIATION EXPENSE C. S. EQUIPMENT ACCOUNT NO. 5080

Date	Explanation	Post Ref.	Debit	Credit	Balance Debit	Balance Credit

DEPRECIATION EXPENSE OFFICE EQUIPMENT ACCOUNT NO. 5090

Date	Explanation	Post Ref.	Debit	Credit	Balance Debit	Balance Credit

MISCELLANEOUS EXPENSE ACCOUNT NO. 5100

Date	Explanation	Post Ref.	Debit	Credit	Balance Debit	Balance Credit
10/31 0X	Balance forward	✔			1 0 00	

WAGES EXPENSE ACCOUNT NO. 5110

Date	Explanation	Post Ref.	Debit	Credit	Balance Debit	Balance Credit

(2) Use the fold-out payroll register that accompanied your textbook.

SANCHEZ COMPUTER CENTER
TRIAL BALANCE
NOVEMBER 30, 200X

		Dr.	Cr.

8
The Employer's Tax Responsibilities: Principles and Procedures

SELF-REVIEW QUIZ 8-1

GENERAL JOURNAL

PAGE 1

Date	Account Titles and Description	PR	Dr.	Cr.

Name _____ Class _____ Date _____

SELF-REVIEW QUIZ 8-2

1.

2.

SELF-REVIEW QUIZ 8-3

1. _____ 2. _____ 3. _____ 4. _____ 5. _____ 6. _____

CHAPTER 8

SET A **FORMS FOR CLASSROOM DEMONSTRATION EXERCISES**

1.

A. B. C. D. E.			

2.
   A. _____
   B. _____
   C. _____
   D. _____

3.
   _____
   _____
   _____
   _____

4.
   A. _____
   B. _____
   C. _____
   D. _____
   E. _____
   F. _____
   G. _____

5.
   A. _____
   B. _____
   C. _____
   D. _____
   E. _____

SG-235

Name _____ Class _____ Date _____

CHAPTER 8
SET B   **FORMS FOR CLASSROOM DEMONSTRATION EXERCISES**

1.

A. B. C. D. E.			

2.
 A. _____
 B. _____
 C. _____
 D. _____

3.
 _____
 _____
 _____
 _____

4.
 A. _____
 B. _____
 C. _____
 D. _____
 E. _____
 F. _____
 G. _____

5.
 A. _____
 B. _____
 C. _____
 D. _____
 E. _____

Name _____ Class _____ Date _____

FORMS FOR EXERCISES

8-1.

ACCOUNT	CATEGORY	DR/CR	STATEMENT FOUND ON

8-2.

8-3.

SG-237

EXERCISES (CONCLUDED)

8-4.

8-5.

8-6.

8-7.

8-8.

END OF CHAPTER PROBLEMS

PROBLEM 8A-1 OR PROBLEM 8B-1

Employee	Allowance & Marital Status	Gross	FICA		Federal Income Tax
			OASDI	Medicare	

(2)

PROBLEM 8A-2 OR PROBLEM 8B-2

Date	Account Titles and Description	PR	Dr.	Cr.

PROBLEM 8A-2 OR PROBLEM 8B-2 (CONCLUDED)

Date	Account Titles and Description	PR	Dr.	Cr.

Name _____ Class _____ Date _____

PROBLEM 8A-3 OR PROBLEM 8B-3

Form **941 for 200X:** Employer's QUARTERLY Federal Tax Return
(Rev. January 2006)   Department of the Treasury — Internal Revenue Service

990106
OMB No. 1545-0029

(EIN)
Employer identification number ☐☐ – ☐☐☐☐☐☐☐

Name *(not your trade name)* _____

Trade name *(if any)* _____

Address _____
Number   Street   Suite or room number
City   State   ZIP code

Report for this Quarter ...
(Check one.)
☐ 1: January, February, March
☐ 2: April, May, June
☐ 3: July, August, September
☐ 4: October, November, December

Read the separate instructions before you fill out this form. Please type or print within the boxes.

Part 1: Answer these questions for this quarter.

1. Number of employees who received wages, tips, or other compensation for the pay period including: *Mar. 12* (Quarter 1), *June 12* (Quarter 2), *Sept. 12* (Quarter 3), *Dec. 12* (Quarter 4)   **1** _____

2. Wages, tips, and other compensation . . . . **2** _____

3. Total income tax withheld from wages, tips, and other compensation . . . . . **3** _____

4. If no wages, tips, and other compensation are subject to social security or Medicare tax . . ☐ Check and go to line 6.

5. Taxable social security and Medicare wages and tips:

	Column 1		Column 2
5a Taxable social security wages	_____	× .124 =	_____
5b Taxable social security tips	_____	× .124 =	_____
5c Taxable Medicare wages & tips	_____	× .029 =	_____

   5d Total social security and Medicare taxes (*Column 2,* lines 5a + 5b + 5c = line 5d) . **5d** _____

6. Total taxes before adjustments (lines 3 + 5d = line 6) . . . . **6** _____

7. **TAX ADJUSTMENTS** (Read the instructions for line 7 before completing lines 7a through 7h.):

   7a Current quarter's fractions of cents . . . . _____

   7b Current quarter's sick pay . . . . _____

   7c Current quarter's adjustments for tips and group-term life insurance _____

   7d Current year's income tax withholding (attach Form 941c) . . . _____

   7e Prior quarters' social security and Medicare taxes (attach Form 941c) _____

   7f Special additions to federal income tax (attach Form 941c) . . . _____

   7g Special additions to social security and Medicare (attach Form 941c) _____

   7h **TOTAL ADJUSTMENTS** (Combine all amounts: lines 7a through 7g.) . . . **7h** _____

8. Total taxes after adjustments (Combine lines 6 and 7h.) . . . . **8** _____

9. Advance earned income credit (EIC) payments made to employees . . . . **9** _____

10. Total taxes after adjustment for advance EIC (line 8 – line 9 = line 10) . . . . **10** _____

11. Total deposits for this quarter, including overpayment applied from a prior quarter . . **11** _____

12. Balance due (If line 10 is more than line 11, write the difference here.) . . . . . . **12** _____
    Make checks payable to *United States Treasury.*

13. Overpayment (If line 11 is more than line 10, write the difference here.) _____ Check one ☐ Apply to next return.
                                                                                     ☐ Send a refund.

▶ You **MUST** fill out both pages of this form and **SIGN** it.

Next ➡

For Privacy Act and Paperwork Reduction Act Notice, see the back of the Payment Voucher.   Cat. No. 17001Z   Form **941** (Rev. 1-2006)

Name _____ Class _____ Date _____

PROBLEM 8A-3 OR PROBLEM 8B-3 (CONCLUDED)

990206

Name *(not your trade name)* | **Employer identification number (EIN)**

Part 2: Tell us about your deposit schedule and tax liability for this quarter.

If you are unsure about whether you are a monthly schedule depositor or a semiweekly schedule depositor, see *Pub. 15 (Circular E)*, section 11.

14 ☐☐ Write the state abbreviation for the state where you made your deposits OR write "MU" if you made your deposits in *multiple* states.

15 Check one: ☐ Line 10 is less than $2,500. Go to Part 3.

☐ You were a monthly schedule depositor for the entire quarter. Fill out your tax liability for each month. Then go to Part 3.

Tax liability: Month 1 _____.
Month 2 _____.
Month 3 _____.
Total liability for quarter _____. Total must equal line 10.

☐ You were a semiweekly schedule depositor for any part of this quarter. Fill out *Schedule B (Form 941): Report of Tax Liability for Semiweekly Schedule Depositors*, and attach it to this form.

Part 3: Tell us about your business. If a question does NOT apply to your business, leave it blank.

16 If your business has closed or you stopped paying wages . . . . ☐ Check here, and
enter the final date you paid wages ___/___/___.

17 If you are a seasonal employer and you do not have to file a return for every quarter of the year . ☐ Check here.

Part 4: May we speak with your third-party designee?

Do you want to allow an employee, a paid tax preparer, or another person to discuss this return with the IRS? See the instructions for details.

☐ Yes. Designee's name _____

Phone (___) ___ - ____   Personal Identification Number (PIN) ☐☐☐☐☐

☐ No.

Part 5: Sign here. You MUST fill out both sides of this form and SIGN it.

Under penalties of perjury, I declare that I have examined this return, including accompanying schedules and statements, and to the best of my knowledge and belief, it is true, correct, and complete.

X Sign your name here _____
Print name and title _____
Date ___/___/___   Phone (___) ___ - ____

Part 6: For PAID preparers only *(optional)*

Paid Preparer's Signature _____
Firm's name _____
Address _____   EIN _____
_____   ZIP code _____
Date ___/___/___   Phone (___) ___ - ____   SSN/PTIN _____
☐ Check if you are self-employed.

Page 2   Form **941** (Rev. 1-2006)

SG-243

PROBLEM 8A-4 OR PROBLEM 8B-4

Name _____ Class _____ Date _____

PROBLEM 8A-4 OR PROBLEM 8B-4 (CONTINUED)

Form **941 for 200X**: Employer's QUARTERLY Federal Tax Return
(Rev. January 2006) — Department of the Treasury — Internal Revenue Service

990106
OMB No. 1545-0029

(EIN) Employer identification number ☐☐ – ☐☐☐☐☐☐☐

Name *(not your trade name)*

Trade name *(if any)*

Address — Number, Street, Suite or room number, City, State, ZIP code

Report for this Quarter ... *(Check one.)*
- ☐ 1: January, February, March
- ☐ 2: April, May, June
- ☐ 3: July, August, September
- ☐ 4: October, November, December

Read the separate instructions before you fill out this form. Please type or print within the boxes.

Part 1: Answer these questions for this quarter.

1. Number of employees who received wages, tips, or other compensation for the pay period including: *Mar. 12* (Quarter 1), *June 12* (Quarter 2), *Sept. 12* (Quarter 3), *Dec. 12* (Quarter 4) ... **1** _____

2. Wages, tips, and other compensation ... **2** _____

3. Total income tax withheld from wages, tips, and other compensation ... **3** _____

4. If no wages, tips, and other compensation are subject to social security or Medicare tax ... ☐ Check and go to line 6.

5. Taxable social security and Medicare wages and tips:

	Column 1		Column 2
5a Taxable social security wages	_____	× .124 =	_____
5b Taxable social security tips	_____	× .124 =	_____
5c Taxable Medicare wages & tips	_____	× .029 =	_____

5d Total social security and Medicare taxes (Column 2, lines 5a + 5b + 5c = line 5d) ... **5d** _____

6. Total taxes before adjustments (lines 3 + 5d = line 6) ... **6** _____

7. TAX ADJUSTMENTS (Read the instructions for line 7 before completing lines 7a through 7h.):

   - 7a Current quarter's fractions of cents ... _____
   - 7b Current quarter's sick pay ... _____
   - 7c Current quarter's adjustments for tips and group-term life insurance ... _____
   - 7d Current year's income tax withholding (attach Form 941c) ... _____
   - 7e Prior quarters' social security and Medicare taxes (attach Form 941c) ... _____
   - 7f Special additions to federal income tax (attach Form 941c) ... _____
   - 7g Special additions to social security and Medicare (attach Form 941c) ... _____

   7h TOTAL ADJUSTMENTS (Combine all amounts: lines 7a through 7g.) ... **7h** _____

8. Total taxes after adjustments (Combine lines 6 and 7h.) ... **8** _____

9. Advance earned income credit (EIC) payments made to employees ... **9** _____

10. Total taxes after adjustment for advance EIC (line 8 – line 9 = line 10) ... **10** _____

11. Total deposits for this quarter, including overpayment applied from a prior quarter ... **11** _____

12. Balance due (If line 10 is more than line 11, write the difference here.) ... **12** _____
    Make checks payable to *United States Treasury*.

13. Overpayment (If line 11 is more than line 10, write the difference here.) _____ Check one ☐ Apply to next return. ☐ Send a refund.

▶ You MUST fill out both pages of this form and SIGN it.

Next ➡

For Privacy Act and Paperwork Reduction Act Notice, see the back of the Payment Voucher.   Cat. No. 17001Z   Form **941** (Rev. 1-2006)

SG-245

Name _____ Class _____ Date _____

PROBLEM 8A-4 OR PROBLEM 8B-4 (CONCLUDED)   990206

Name *(not your trade name)* | **Employer identification number (EIN)**

Part 2: Tell us about your deposit schedule and tax liability for this quarter.

If you are unsure about whether you are a monthly schedule depositor or a semiweekly schedule depositor, see *Pub. 15 (Circular E)*, section 11.

14 ☐☐ Write the state abbreviation for the state where you made your deposits OR write "MU" if you made your deposits in *multiple* states.

15 Check one: ☐ Line 10 is less than $2,500. Go to Part 3.

☐ You were a monthly schedule depositor for the entire quarter. Fill out your tax liability for each month. Then go to Part 3.

Tax liability: Month 1 _____
Month 2 _____
Month 3 _____
Total liability for quarter _____ Total must equal line 10.

☐ You were a semiweekly schedule depositor for any part of this quarter. Fill out *Schedule B (Form 941): Report of Tax Liability for Semiweekly Schedule Depositors*, and attach it to this form.

Part 3: Tell us about your business. If a question does NOT apply to your business, leave it blank.

16 If your business has closed or you stopped paying wages . . . . ☐ Check here, and
enter the final date you paid wages ___/___/___ .

17 If you are a seasonal employer and you do not have to file a return for every quarter of the year . . ☐ Check here.

Part 4: May we speak with your third-party designee?

Do you want to allow an employee, a paid tax preparer, or another person to discuss this return with the IRS? See the instructions for details.

☐ Yes. Designee's name _____

Phone (___) ___ - ____ Personal Identification Number (PIN) ☐☐☐☐☐

☐ No.

Part 5: Sign here. You MUST fill out both sides of this form and SIGN it.

Under penalties of perjury, I declare that I have examined this return, including accompanying schedules and statements, and to the best of my knowledge and belief, it is true, correct, and complete.

✗ Sign your name here _____

Print name and title _____

Date ___/___/___   Phone (___) ___ - ____

Part 6: For PAID preparers only *(optional)*

Paid Preparer's Signature _____

Firm's name _____

Address _____   EIN _____

_____   ZIP code _____

Date ___/___/___   Phone (___) ___ - ____   SSN/PTIN _____

☐ Check if you are self-employed.

Page **2**   Form **941** (Rev. 1-2006)

SG-246

Name _____ Class _____ Date _____

PROBLEM 8A-5 OR PROBLEM 8B-5

Form **940 for 200X:** Employer's Annual Federal Unemployment (FUTA) Tax Return 850108
Department of the Treasury — Internal Revenue Service
OMB No. 1545-0028

(EIN) Employer identification number ☐☐ – ☐☐☐☐☐☐☐

Name (not your trade name) _____

Trade name (if any) _____

Address
Number / Street / Suite or room number
City / State / ZIP code

Type of Return
(Check all that apply.)
☐ a. Amended
☐ b. Successor employer
☐ c. No payments to employees in 2008
☐ d. Final: Business closed or stopped paying wages

Read the separate instructions before you fill out this form. Please type or print within the boxes.

Part 1: Tell us about your return. If any line does NOT apply, leave it blank.

1 If you were required to pay your state unemployment tax in ...

   1a One state only, write the state abbreviation .... 1a ☐☐
   - OR -
   1b More than one state (You are a multi-state employer) .... 1b ☐ Check here. Fill out Schedule A.

   Skip line 2 for 2008 and go to line 3.
2 If you paid wages in a state that is subject to CREDIT REDUCTION .... 2 ☐ Check here. Fill out Schedule A (Form 940), Part 2.

Part 2: Determine your FUTA tax before adjustments for 2008. If any line does NOT apply, leave it blank.

3 Total payments to all employees .... 3 _____ .

4 Payments exempt from FUTA tax .... 4 _____ .

   Check all that apply: **4a** ☐ Fringe benefits   **4c** ☐ Retirement/Pension   **4e** ☐ Other
                        4b ☐ Group-term life insurance   **4d** ☐ Dependent care

5 Total of payments made to each employee in excess of $7,000 .... 5 _____ .

6 Subtotal (line 4 + line 5 = line 6) .... 6 _____ .

7 Total taxable FUTA wages (line 3 – line 6 = line 7) .... 7 _____ .

8 FUTA tax before adjustments (line 7 × .008 = line 8) .... 8 _____ .

Part 3: Determine your adjustments. If any line does NOT apply, leave it blank.

9 If ALL of the taxable FUTA wages you paid were excluded from state unemployment tax, multiply line 7 by .054 (line 7 × .054 = line 9). Then go to line 12 .... 9 _____ .

10 If SOME of the taxable FUTA wages you paid were excluded from state unemployment tax, OR you paid ANY state unemployment tax late (after the due date for filing Form 940), fill out the worksheet in the instructions. Enter the amount from line 7 of the worksheet onto line 10 .. 10 _____ .

   Skip line 11 for 2008 and go to line 12.
11 If credit reduction applies, enter the amount from line 3 of Schedule A (Form 940) ..... 11 _____ .

Part 4: Determine your FUTA tax and balance due or overpayment for 2008. If any line does NOT apply, leave it blank.

12 Total FUTA tax after adjustments (lines 8 + 9 + 10 + 11 = line 12) .... 12 _____ .

13 FUTA tax deposited for the year, including any payment applied from a prior year .... 13 _____ .

14 **Balance due** (If line 12 is more than line 13, enter the difference on line 14.)
   • If line 14 is more than $500, you must deposit your tax.
   • If line 14 is $500 or less, you may pay with this return. For more information on how to pay, see the separate instructions .... 14 _____ .

15 **Overpayment** (If line 13 is more than line 12, enter the difference on line 15 and check a box below.) .... 15 _____ .

   Check one: ☐ Apply to next return.
             ☐ Send a refund.

▶ You **MUST** fill out both pages of this form and **SIGN** it.

Next ➡

For Privacy Act and Paperwork Reduction Act Notice, see the back of Form 940-V, Payment Voucher. Cat. No. 11234O Form **940** (2008)

Name _____ Class _____ Date _____

PROBLEM 8A-5 OR PROBLEM 8B-5 (CONCLUDED)

Name *(not your trade name)* | **Employer identification number (EIN)**

Part 5: Report your FUTA tax liability by quarter only if line 12 is more than $500. If not, go to Part 6.

16 Report the amount of your FUTA tax liability for each quarter; do NOT enter the amount you deposited. If you had no liability for a quarter, leave the line blank.

- 16a 1st quarter (January 1 – March 31) . . . . 16a [.   ]
- 16b 2nd quarter (April 1 – June 30) . . . . 16b [.   ]
- 16c 3rd quarter (July 1 – September 30) . . . . 16c [.   ]
- 16d 4th quarter (October 1 – December 31) . . . . 16d [.   ]

17 Total tax liability for the year (lines 16a + 16b + 16c + 16d = line 17) 17 [.   ]   Total must equal line 12.

Part 6: May we speak with your third-party designee?

Do you want to allow an employee, a paid tax preparer, or another person to discuss this return with the IRS? See the instructions for details.

☐ **Yes.** Designee's name and phone number [   ] ( ) –

Select a 5-digit Personal Identification Number (PIN) to use when talking to IRS [ ][ ][ ][ ][ ]

☐ **No.**

Part 7: Sign here. You MUST fill out both pages of this form and SIGN it.

Under penalties of perjury, I declare that I have examined this return, including accompanying schedules and statements, and to the best of my knowledge and belief, it is true, correct, and complete, and that no part of any payment made to a state unemployment fund claimed as a credit was, or is to be, deducted from the payments made to employees. Declaration of preparer (other than taxpayer) is based on all information of which preparer has any knowledge.

✗ **Sign your name here** [   ]   Print your name here [   ]

Print your title here [   ]

Date __ / __ / __   Best daytime phone ( ) –

Paid preparer's use only   Check if you are self-employed . . . ☐

Preparer's name [   ]   Preparer's SSN/PTIN [   ]

Preparer's signature [   ]   Date __ / __ / __

Firm's name (or yours if self-employed) [   ]   EIN [   ]

Address [   ]   Phone ( ) –

City [   ]   State [   ]   ZIP code [   ]

Page 2   Form **940** (2008)

SG-248

Name _____ Class _____ Date _____

CHAPTER 8
SUMMARY PRACTICE TEST:
THE EMPLOYER'S TAX RESPONSIBILITIES:
PRINCIPLES AND PROCEDURES

Part I Instructions

Fill in the blank(s) to complete the statement.

1. Form 941 is completed _____.
2. The payroll tax expense for the employer is made up of _____, _____, and FUTA.
3. Data from the _____ _____ will provide the needed information to record the payroll in the general journal.
4. SUTA is usually paid _____.
5. FUTA Payable is a _____ found on the _____ _____.
6. Form 941 summarizes the taxes owed for _____ and _____.
7. _____ _____ _____ will tell if a deposit is to be made monthly or semiweekly for FIT and Social Security.
8. Form _____ is prepared quarterly to summarize tax liabilities for FICA (Social Security and Medicare) and FIT.
9. The _____ _____ _____ _____ is required to be given to employees by January 31 following the year employed.
10. _____ does not have a merit rating like SUTA.

Part II Instructions

Answer true or false to the following.

1. Prepaid Workers' Compensation Insurance is a liability.
2. Payroll taxes are recorded as assets for a business.
3. Payroll Tax Expense is made up of FICA, SUTA, and FIT.
4. Frequency of deposits relating to Form 941 is based on amount of tax liability in look-back periods.
5. The normal balance of FIT payable is a debit.
6. The individual earnings record provides the data to prepare W-2s.
7. A tax calendar provides little help to the employer involving the payment of tax liabilities.
8. Form 941 is completed twice a year.
9. A year-end adjusting entry is needed for workers' compensation.
10. Form 8109 relates only to Form 940.

SG-249

Name _____ Class _____ Date _____

Part III Instructions

Complete the following table:

ACCOUNT	CATEGORY	FOUND ON WHICH REPORT
1. Salaries Payable		
2. FUTA Payable		
3. SUTA Payable		
4. OASDI Tax Payable—Medicare		
5. FIT Payable		
6. Office Salaries Expense		

Part IV Instructions

Complete the following table:

	4 QUARTERS LOOK-BACK PERIOD LIABILITY	PAYROLL PAID WEEKLY	TAX PAID BY:
Sit. A	$40,000	October	?
Sit. B	75,000		
		on Wed.	?
		on Thurs.	?
		on Fri	?
		on Sat.	?
		on Sun.	?
		on Mon.	?
		on Tues.	?

Why is the depositor in situation A classified as a monthly depositor while in situation B the depositor is classified as semiweekly?

SOLUTIONS TO SUMMARY PRACTICE TEST

Part I

1. quarterly
2. FICA (OASDI and Medicare), SUTA
3. payroll register
4. quarterly
5. liability, balance sheet
6. FICA (OASDI and Medicare), FIT
7. Look-back periods
8. 941
9. Wage and Tax Statement
10. FUTA

Part II

1. false
2. false
3. false
4. true
5. false
6. true
7. false
8. false
9. true
10. false

Part III

1. Liability; Balance Sheet
2. Liability; Balance Sheet
3. Liability; Balance Sheet
4. Liability; Balance Sheet
5. Liability; Balance Sheet
6. Expense; Income Statement

Part IV

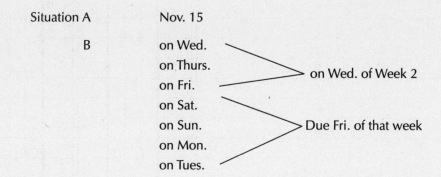

The depositor in situation A is classified as a monthly depositor because its tax liability of $40,000 during the look-back period was less than the $50,000 limit.

On the other hand, the depositor in situation B owed $75,000 during the look-back period. Since this is greater than the $50,000 limit, it was classified as a semiweekly depositor.

CONTINUING PROBLEM FOR CHAPTER 8
SANCHEZ COMPUTER CENTER

SANCHEZ COMPUTER CENTER
GENERAL JOURNAL

PAGE 5

Date	Account Titles and Description	PR	Dr.	Cr.

CONTINUING PROBLEM FOR CHAPTER 8
SANCHEZ COMPUTER CENTER

SANCHEZ COMPUTER CENTER
GENERAL JOURNAL

PAGE 6

Date	Account Titles and Description	PR	Dr.	Cr.

Name _____ Class _____ Date _____

CONTINUING PROBLEM FOR CHAPTER 8
SANCHEZ COMPUTER CENTER

Form **941 for 200X:** Employer's QUARTERLY Federal Tax Return
(Rev. January 2006)   Department of the Treasury — Internal Revenue Service

990106
OMB No. 1545-0029

(EIN) Employer identification number ☐☐ – ☐☐☐☐☐☐☐

Name *(not your trade name)* _____

Trade name *(if any)* _____

Address
Number _____ Street _____ Suite or room number _____
City _____ State _____ ZIP code _____

Report for this Quarter ...
(Check one.)
☐ 1: January, February, March
☐ 2: April, May, June
☐ 3: July, August, September
☐ 4: October, November, December

Read the separate instructions before you fill out this form. Please type or print within the boxes.

Part 1: Answer these questions for this quarter.

1 Number of employees who received wages, tips, or other compensation for the pay period including: *Mar. 12* (Quarter 1), *June 12* (Quarter 2), *Sept. 12* (Quarter 3), *Dec. 12* (Quarter 4)   **1** ☐

2 Wages, tips, and other compensation . . . .   **2** ☐

3 Total income tax withheld from wages, tips, and other compensation . . . . . .   **3** ☐

4 If no wages, tips, and other compensation are subject to social security or Medicare tax . .   ☐ Check and go to line 6.

5 Taxable social security and Medicare wages and tips:

	Column 1		Column 2
5a Taxable social security wages	☐	× .124 =	☐
5b Taxable social security tips	☐	× .124 =	☐
5c Taxable Medicare wages & tips	☐	× .029 =	☐

5d Total social security and Medicare taxes (*Column 2*, lines 5a + 5b + 5c = line 5d)   **5d** ☐

6 Total taxes before adjustments (lines 3 + 5d = line 6) . . . .   **6** ☐

7 **TAX ADJUSTMENTS** (Read the instructions for line 7 before completing lines 7a through 7h.):

7a Current quarter's fractions of cents . . . . ☐
7b Current quarter's sick pay . . . . ☐
7c Current quarter's adjustments for tips and group-term life insurance ☐
7d Current year's income tax withholding (attach Form 941c) . . ☐
7e Prior quarters' social security and Medicare taxes (attach Form 941c) ☐
7f Special additions to federal income tax (attach Form 941c) . . ☐
7g Special additions to social security and Medicare (attach Form 941c) ☐

7h **TOTAL ADJUSTMENTS** (Combine all amounts: lines 7a through 7g.) . . . . .   **7h** ☐

8 Total taxes after adjustments (Combine lines 6 and 7h.) . . . .   **8** ☐

9 Advance earned income credit (EIC) payments made to employees . . . . . .   **9** ☐

10 Total taxes after adjustment for advance EIC (line 8 – line 9 = line 10) . . . . .   **10** ☐

11 Total deposits for this quarter, including overpayment applied from a prior quarter . . .   **11** ☐

12 **Balance due** (If line 10 is more than line 11, write the difference here.) . . . . . .   **12** ☐
Make checks payable to *United States Treasury*.

13 **Overpayment** (If line 11 is more than line 10, write the difference here.) ☐   Check one ☐ Apply to next return.
☐ Send a refund.

▶ You **MUST** fill out both pages of this form and **SIGN** it.

Next ➡

For Privacy Act and Paperwork Reduction Act Notice, see the back of the Payment Voucher.   Cat. No. 17001Z   Form **941** (Rev. 1-2006)

Name _____ Class _____ Date _____

CONTINUING PROBLEM FOR CHAPTER 8
SANCHEZ COMPUTER CENTER

990206

Name *(not your trade name)* | **Employer identification number (EIN)**

Part 2: Tell us about your deposit schedule and tax liability for this quarter.

If you are unsure about whether you are a monthly schedule depositor or a semiweekly schedule depositor, see *Pub. 15 (Circular E)*, section 11.

14 ☐☐ Write the state abbreviation for the state where you made your deposits OR write "MU" if you made your deposits in *multiple* states.

15 Check one: ☐ Line 10 is less than $2,500. Go to Part 3.

☐ You were a monthly schedule depositor for the entire quarter. Fill out your tax liability for each month. Then go to Part 3.

Tax liability: Month 1 _____
Month 2 _____
Month 3 _____

Total liability for quarter _____ Total must equal line 10.

☐ You were a semiweekly schedule depositor for any part of this quarter. Fill out *Schedule B (Form 941): Report of Tax Liability for Semiweekly Schedule Depositors,* and attach it to this form.

Part 3: Tell us about your business. If a question does NOT apply to your business, leave it blank.

16 If your business has closed or you stopped paying wages . . . . ☐ Check here, and

enter the final date you paid wages ____/____/____.

17 If you are a seasonal employer and you do not have to file a return for every quarter of the year . . ☐ Check here.

Part 4: May we speak with your third-party designee?

Do you want to allow an employee, a paid tax preparer, or another person to discuss this return with the IRS? See the instructions for details.

☐ Yes. Designee's name _____

Phone (___) ___ - _____ Personal Identification Number (PIN) ☐☐☐☐☐

☐ No.

Part 5: Sign here. You MUST fill out both sides of this form and SIGN it.

Under penalties of perjury, I declare that I have examined this return, including accompanying schedules and statements, and to the best of my knowledge and belief, it is true, correct, and complete.

✗ Sign your name here _____

Print name and title _____

Date ____/____/____ Phone (___) ___ - _____

Part 6: For PAID preparers only *(optional)*

Paid Preparer's Signature _____

Firm's name _____

Address _____ EIN _____

_____ ZIP code _____

Date ____/____/____ Phone (___) ___ - _____ SSN/PTIN _____

☐ Check if you are self-employed.

Page **2** Form **941** (Rev. 1-2006)

Name _____ Class _____ Date _____

Form **940 for 200X:** Employer's Annual Federal Unemployment (FUTA) Tax Return   850108
Department of the Treasury — Internal Revenue Service
OMB No. 1545-0028

(EIN) Employer identification number ☐☐ – ☐☐☐☐☐☐☐

Name *(not your trade name)*

Trade name *(if any)*

Address
Number Street
Suite or room number
City State ZIP code

Type of Return
(Check all that apply.)
☐ a. Amended
☐ b. Successor employer
☐ c. No payments to employees in 2008
☐ d. Final: Business closed or stopped paying wages

Read the separate instructions before you fill out this form. Please type or print within the boxes.

Part 1: Tell us about your return. If any line does NOT apply, leave it blank.

1 If you were required to pay your state unemployment tax in ...

   1a One state only, write the state abbreviation . . . . 1a ☐☐
   - OR -
   1b More than one state (You are a multi-state employer) . . . . 1b ☐ Check here. Fill out Schedule A.

   Skip line 2 for 2008 and go to line 3.

2 If you paid wages in a state that is subject to CREDIT REDUCTION . . . . 2 ☐ Check here. Fill out Schedule A (Form 940), Part 2.

Part 2: Determine your FUTA tax before adjustments for 2008. If any line does NOT apply, leave it blank.

3 Total payments to all employees . . . . 3 ☐

4 Payments exempt from FUTA tax . . . . 4 ☐

   Check all that apply: 4a ☐ Fringe benefits   4c ☐ Retirement/Pension   4e ☐ Other
   4b ☐ Group-term life insurance   4d ☐ Dependent care

5 Total of payments made to each employee in excess of $7,000 . . . . 5 ☐

6 **Subtotal** (line 4 + line 5 = line 6) . . . . 6 ☐

7 **Total taxable FUTA wages** (line 3 – line 6 = line 7) . . . . 7 ☐

8 **FUTA tax before adjustments** (line 7 × .008 = line 8) . . . . 8 ☐

Part 3: Determine your adjustments. If any line does NOT apply, leave it blank.

9 If ALL of the taxable FUTA wages you paid were excluded from state unemployment tax, multiply line 7 by .054 (line 7 × .054 = line 9). Then go to line 12 . . . . 9 ☐

10 If SOME of the taxable FUTA wages you paid were excluded from state unemployment tax, OR you paid ANY state unemployment tax late (after the due date for filing Form 940), fill out the worksheet in the instructions. Enter the amount from line 7 of the worksheet onto line 10 . . 10 ☐

   Skip line 11 for 2008 and go to line 12.

11 If credit reduction applies, enter the amount from line 3 of Schedule A (Form 940) . . . . . 11 ☐

Part 4: Determine your FUTA tax and balance due or overpayment for 2008. If any line does NOT apply, leave it blank.

12 **Total FUTA tax after adjustments** (lines 8 + 9 + 10 + 11 = line 12) . . . . 12 ☐

13 FUTA tax deposited for the year, including any payment applied from a prior year . . . . 13 ☐

14 **Balance due** (If line 12 is more than line 13, enter the difference on line 14.)
   • If line 14 is more than $500, you must deposit your tax.
   • If line 14 is $500 or less, you may pay with this return. For more information on how to pay, see the separate instructions . . . . 14 ☐

15 **Overpayment** (If line 13 is more than line 12, enter the difference on line 15 and check a box below.) . . . . 15 ☐

   Check one: ☐ Apply to next return.
   ☐ Send a refund.

▶ You **MUST** fill out both pages of this form and **SIGN** it.

Next ➡

For Privacy Act and Paperwork Reduction Act Notice, see the back of Form 940-V, Payment Voucher.   Cat. No. 112340   Form **940** (2008)

SG-256

Name _____ Class _____ Date _____

Name *(not your trade name)* _____ | Employer identification number (EIN) _____

Part 5: Report your FUTA tax liability by quarter only if line 12 is more than $500. If not, go to Part 6.

16 Report the amount of your FUTA tax liability for each quarter; do NOT enter the amount you deposited. If you had no liability for a quarter, leave the line blank.

    16a   1st quarter (January 1 – March 31) . . . . 16a [.   ]

    16b   2nd quarter (April 1 – June 30) . . . . 16b [.   ]

    16c   3rd quarter (July 1 – September 30) . . . . 16c [.   ]

    16d   4th quarter (October 1 – December 31) . . . . 16d [.   ]

17 Total tax liability for the year (lines 16a + 16b + 16c + 16d = line 17) 17 [.   ] Total must equal line 12.

Part 6: May we speak with your third-party designee?

Do you want to allow an employee, a paid tax preparer, or another person to discuss this return with the IRS? See the instructions for details.

☐ **Yes.** Designee's name and phone number [_____] (   )   –

         Select a 5-digit Personal Identification Number (PIN) to use when talking to IRS [ ][ ][ ][ ][ ]

☐ **No.**

Part 7: Sign here. You MUST fill out both pages of this form and SIGN it.

Under penalties of perjury, I declare that I have examined this return, including accompanying schedules and statements, and to the best of my knowledge and belief, it is true, correct, and complete, and that no part of any payment made to a state unemployment fund claimed as a credit was, or is to be, deducted from the payments made to employees. Declaration of preparer (other than taxpayer) is based on all information of which preparer has any knowledge.

✗ **Sign your name here** [_____]

    Print your name here [_____]

    Print your title here [_____]

    Date [/   /   ]   Best daytime phone (   )   –

Paid preparer's use only   Check if you are self-employed . . . ☐

Preparer's name [_____]   Preparer's SSN/PTIN [_____]

Preparer's signature [_____]   Date [/   /   ]

Firm's name (or yours if self-employed) [_____]   EIN [_____]

Address [_____]   Phone (   )   –

City [_____]   State [_____]   ZIP code [_____]

9

Sales and Cash Receipts

SELF-REVIEW QUIZ 9-1

1. _____ 2. _____ 3. _____ 4. _____ 5. _____

SELF-REVIEW QUIZ 9-2

BERNIE COMPANY
GENERAL JOURNAL

PAGE 1

Date	Account Titles and Description	PR	Dr.	Cr.

ACCOUNTS RECEIVABLE SUBSIDIARY LEDGER

NAME   LEE CORP.
ADDRESS   118 MORRIS RD., BOSTON, MA 01935

Date	Explanation	Post Ref.	Debit	Credit	Dr. Balance

NAME   RING COMPANY
ADDRESS   31 NORRIS ROAD, BOSTON, MA 01935

Date	Explanation	Post Ref.	Debit	Credit	Dr. Balance

PARTIAL GENERAL LEDGER

ACCOUNT RECEIVABLE   **ACCOUNT NO. 141**

Date	Explanation	Post Ref.	Debit	Credit	Balance Debit	Balance Credit

SALES   **ACCOUNT NO. 310**

Date	Explanation	Post Ref.	Debit	Credit	Balance Debit	Balance Credit

SALES RETURNS AND ALLOWANCES   **ACCOUNT NO. 312**

Date	Explanation	Post Ref.	Debit	Credit	Balance Debit	Balance Credit

SELF-REVIEW QUIZ 9-3

MABEL CORPORATION
GENERAL JOURNAL

PAGE 3

Date	Account Titles and Description	PR	Dr.	Cr.

PARTIAL GENERAL LEDGER

CASH   ACCOUNT NO. 110

Date 200X	Explanation	Post Ref.	Debit	Credit	Balance Debit	Balance Credit
May 1	Balance	✓			600 00	

ACCOUNTS RECEIVABLE   ACCOUNT NO. 120

Date 200X	Explanation	Post Ref.	Debit	Credit	Balance Debit	Balance Credit
May 1	Balance	✓			700 00	

STORE EQUIPMENT   ACCOUNT NO. 130

Date 200X	Explanation	Post Ref.	Debit	Credit	Balance Debit	Balance Credit
May 1	Balance	✓			600 00	

SALES   ACCOUNT NO. 410

Date 200X	Explanation	Post Ref.	Debit	Credit	Balance Debit	Balance Credit
May 1	Balance	✓				700 00

Name _____ Class _____ Date _____

SALES DISCOUNT   ACCOUNT NO. 420

Date 200X	Explanation	Post Ref.	Debit	Credit	Balance Debit	Balance Credit

NAME   JANIS FROSS
ADDRESS   81 FOSTER RD., BEVERLY, MA 09125

Date 200X	Explanation	Post Ref.	Debit	Credit	Dr. Balance
May 1	Balance	✓			2 0 0 00

ACCOUNTS RECEIVABLE SUBSIDIARY LEDGER

NAME   IRENE WELCH
ADDRESS   10 RONG RD., BEVERLY, MA 01215

Date 200X	Explanation	Post Ref.	Debit	Credit	Dr. Balance
May 1	Balance	✓			5 0 0 00

Name _____ Class _____ Date _____

CHAPTER 9
FORMS FOR CLASSROOM DEMONSTRATION EXERCISES SET A OR SET B

1.

2.

3.
A. _____   _____   _____
B. _____   _____   _____
C. _____   _____   _____

4.

5.

PAGE 6

Date	Account Titles and Description	PR	Dr.	Cr.

6.

BLUE CO.
SCHEDULE OF ACCOUNTS RECEIVABLE
MAY 31, 200X

FORMS FOR EXERCISES

9-1.

Amazon.com	Accounts Receivable 112
Bill Valley Co.	Sales 412

9-2.

GENERAL JOURNAL

PAGE 1

Date	Account Titles and Description	PR	Dr.	Cr.

Bass Co.	Sales 411	
Ronald Co.	Accounts Receivable 112	Sales Returns & Allowances 412

SG-266

EXERCISES (CONTINUED)

9-3.

9-4.

EDNA CO.
GENERAL JOURNAL

PAGE 1

Date	Account Titles and Description	PR	Dr.	Cr.

SG-267

EXERCISES (CONCLUDED)

GENERAL JOURNAL (CONTINUED)   PAGE 1

Date	Account Titles and Description	PR	Dr.	Cr.

ACCOUNTS RECEIVABLE SUBSIDIARY LEDGER   **PARTIAL GENERAL LEDGER**

Boston Co.

Gary Co.

Cash   111

Accounts Receivable   113

Edna Cares, Capital   311

Sales   411

Sales Returns & Allowances   412

Sales Discount   413

EDNA CO.
SCHEDULE OF ACCOUNTS RECEIVABLE
JUNE 30, 200X

9-5.

END OF CHAPTER PROBLEMS

PROBLEM 9A-1 OR PROBLEM 9B-1

PIZZA AND MORE
GENERAL JOURNAL

PAGE 1

Date	Account Titles and Description	PR	Dr.	Cr.

PROBLEM 9A-1 OR PROBLEM 9B-1 (CONTINUED)

ACCOUNTS RECEIVABLE SUBSIDIARY LEDGER

NAME CINDY CO.

ADDRESS 942 MOSE ST., REVERE, MA 01938

Date	Explanation	Post Ref.	Debit	Credit	Dr. Balance

NAME FRENCH CO.

ADDRESS 8 JOSS AVE., LYNN, MA 01947

Date	Explanation	Post Ref.	Debit	Credit	Dr. Balance

NAME GROOM CO.

ADDRESS 10 LOST RD., TOPSFIELD, MA 01998

Date	Explanation	Post Ref.	Debit	Credit	Dr. Balance

Name _____ Class _____ Date _____

PROBLEM 9A-1 OR PROBLEM 9B-1 (CONTINUED)

PIZZA AND MORE
GENERAL LEDGER

ACCOUNTS RECEIVABLE ACCOUNT NO. 112

Date	Explanation	Post Ref.	Debit	Credit	Balance Debit	Balance Credit

PIZZA SALES ACCOUNT NO. 410

Date	Explanation	Post Ref.	Debit	Credit	Balance Debit	Balance Credit

GROCERY SALES ACCOUNT NO. 411

Date	Explanation	Post Ref.	Debit	Credit	Balance Debit	Balance Credit

SALES RETURNS AND ALLOWANCES ACCOUNT NO. 412

Date	Explanation	Post Ref.	Debit	Credit	Balance Debit	Balance Credit

PROBLEM 9A-1 OR PROBLEM 9B-1 (CONCLUDED)

PIZZA AND MORE
SCHEDULE OF ACCOUNTS RECEIVABLE
JUNE 30, 200X

PROBLEM 9A-2 OR PROBLEM 9B-2

TED'S AUTO SUPPLY
GENERAL JOURNAL

PAGE 2

Date	Account Titles and Description	PR	Dr.	Cr.

PROBLEM 9A-2 OR PROBLEM 9B-2 (CONTINUED)

ACCOUNTS RECEIVABLE SUBSIDIARY LEDGER

NAME LANCE CORNER

ADDRESS 9 ROE ST., BARTLETT, NH 01382

Date 200X		Explanation	Post Ref.	Debit	Credit	Dr. Balance
Nov	1	Balance	✔			400 00

NAME J. SETH

ADDRESS 22 REESE ST., LACONIA, NH 04321

Date 200X		Explanation	Post Ref.	Debit	Credit	Dr. Balance
Nov	1	Balance	✔			200 00

NAME R. VOLAN

ADDRESS 12 ASTER RD., MERRIMACK, NH 02134

Date 200X		Explanation	Post Ref.	Debit	Credit	Dr. Balance
Nov	1	Balance	✔			100 00

PROBLEM 9A-2 OR PROBLEM 9B-2 (CONTINUED)

TED'S AUTO SUPPLY
PARTIAL GENERAL LEDGER

ACCOUNTS RECEIVABLE — ACCOUNT NO. 110

Date 200X	Explanation	Post Ref.	Debit	Credit	Balance Debit	Balance Credit
Nov 1	Balance	✓			1 600 00	

SALES TAX PAYABLE — ACCOUNT NO. 210

Date 200X	Explanation	Post Ref.	Debit	Credit	Balance Debit	Balance Credit
Nov 1	Balance	✓				1 600 00

AUTO PARTS SALES — ACCOUNT NO. 410

Date	Explanation	Post Ref.	Debit	Credit	Balance Debit	Balance Credit

SALES RETURNS AND ALLOWANCES — ACCOUNT NO. 420

Date	Explanation	Post Ref.	Debit	Credit	Balance Debit	Balance Credit

Name _____ Class _____ Date _____

PROBLEM 9A-2 OR PROBLEM 9B-2 (CONCLUDED)

(3)

TED'S AUTO SUPPLY
SCHEDULE OF ACCOUNTS RECEIVABLE
NOVEMBER 30, 200X

PROBLEM 9A-3 OR PROBLEM 9B-3
(1,2)

PEAKER'S SNEAKER SHOP
GENERAL JOURNAL

PAGE 2

Date	Account Titles and Description	PR	Dr.	Cr.

PROBLEM 9A-3 OR PROBLEM 9B-3 (CONTINUED)
(1,2)

PEAKER'S SNEAKER SHOP
GENERAL JOURNAL

PAGE 3

Date	Account Titles and Description	PR	Dr.	Cr.

PROBLEM 9A-3 OR PROBLEM 9B-3 (CONTINUED)

ACCOUNTS RECEIVABLE SUBSIDIARY LEDGER

NAME B. DALE
ADDRESS 1822 RIVER RD., MEMPHIS, TN 09111

Date 200X		Explanation	Post Ref.	Debit	Credit	Dr. Balance
May	1	Balance	✓			400 00

NAME RON LESTER
ADDRESS 18 MASS. AVE., SAN DIEGO, CA 01999

Date		Explanation	Post Ref.	Debit	Credit	Dr. Balance
May	1	Balance	✓			800 00

ACCOUNTS RECEIVABLE SUBSIDIARY LEDGER

NAME PAM PRY
ADDRESS 918 MOORE DR., HOMEWOOD, IL 60430

Date 200X		Explanation	Post Ref.	Debit	Credit	Dr. Balance
May	1	Balance	✓			600 00

PROBLEM 9A-3 OR PROBLEM 9B-3 (CONTINUED)

NAME JIM ZON

ADDRESS 2 CHESTNUT ST., SWAMPSCOTT, MA 01970

Date 200X		Explanation	Post Ref.	Debit	Credit	Dr. Balance
May	1	Balance	✔			400 00

PEAKER'S SNEAKER SHOP
PARTIAL GENERAL LEDGER

CASH   **ACCOUNT NO. 10**

Date 200X		Explanation	Post Ref.	Debit	Credit	Balance Debit	Balance Credit
May	1	Balance	✔			15 500 00	

PROBLEM 9A-3 OR PROBLEM 9B-3 (CONTINUED)

ACCOUNTS RECEIVABLE   ACCOUNT NO. 12

Date 200X		Explanation	Post Ref.	Debit	Credit	Balance Debit	Balance Credit
May	1	Balance	✔			2 200 00	

SNEAKER RACK EQUIPMENT   ACCOUNT NO. 14

Date 200X		Explanation	Post Ref.	Debit	Credit	Balance Debit	Balance Credit
May	1	Balance	✔			1 000 00	

MARK PEAKER, CAPITAL   ACCOUNT NO. 30

Date 200X		Explanation	Post Ref.	Debit	Credit	Balance Debit	Balance Credit
May	1	Balance	✔				40 000 00

PROBLEM 9A-3 OR PROBLEM 9B-3 (CONTINUED)

SALES   ACCOUNT NO. 40

Date 200X	Explanation	Post Ref.	Debit	Credit	Balance Debit	Balance Credit
May 1	Balance	✓				2 2 0 0 00

SALES DISCOUNT   ACCOUNT NO. 42

Date 200X	Explanation	Post Ref.	Debit	Credit	Balance Debit	Balance Credit

SALES RETURNS & ALLOWANCES   ACCOUNT NO. 44

Date 200X	Explanation	Post Ref.	Debit	Credit	Balance Debit	Balance Credit

PROBLEM 9A-3 OR PROBLEM 9B-3 (CONCLUDED)

(3)

PEAKER'S SNEAKER SHOP
SCHEDULE OF ACCOUNTS RECEIVABLE
MAY 31, 200X

PROBLEM 9A-4 OR PROBLEM 9B-4

BILL'S COSMETIC MARKET
GENERAL JOURNAL

PAGE 1

Date	Account Titles and Description	PR	Dr.	Cr.

PROBLEM 9A-4 OR PROBLEM 9B-4 (CONTINUED)

BILL'S COSMETIC MARKET
GENERAL JOURNAL

PAGE 2

Date	Account Titles and Description	PR	Dr.	Cr.

Name _____ Class _____ Date _____

PROBLEM 9A-4 OR PROBLEM 9B-4 (CONTINUED)

ACCOUNTS RECEIVABLE SUBSIDIARY LEDGER

NAME   ALICE KOY CO.

ADDRESS   2 RYAN RD., BUFFALO, NY 09113

Date	Explanation	Post Ref.	Debit	Credit	Debit Balance

PROBLEM 9A-4 OR PROBLEM 9B-4 (CONTINUED)

ACCOUNTS RECEIVABLE SUBSIDIARY LEDGER

NAME RUSTY NEAL CO.
ADDRESS 4 REEL RD., LANCASTER, PA 04332

Date	Explanation	Post Ref.	Debit	Credit	Debit Balance

NAME MARIKA SANCHEZ CO.
ADDRESS 14 BONE DR., ENGLEWOOD CLIFFS, NJ 07632

Date	Explanation	Post Ref.	Debit	Credit	Debit Balance

NAME JEFF TONG CO.
ADDRESS 2 MARION RD., BOSTON, MA 01981

Date	Explanation	Post Ref.	Debit	Credit	Debit Balance

Name _____ Class _____ Date _____

PROBLEM 9A-4 OR PROBLEM 9B-4 (CONTINUED)

BILL'S COSMETIC MARKET
GENERAL LEDGER

CASH   ACCOUNT NO. 10

Date	Explanation	Post Ref.	Debit	Credit	Balance Debit	Balance Credit

ACCOUNTS RECEIVABLE   ACCOUNT NO. 12

Date	Explanation	Post Ref.	Debit	Credit	Balance Debit	Balance Credit

PROBLEM 9A-4 OR PROBLEM 9B-4 (CONTINUED)

SALES TAX PAYABLE   ACCOUNT NO. 20

Date	Explanation	Post Ref.	Debit	Credit	Balance Debit	Balance Credit

BILL MURRAY, CAPITAL   ACCOUNT NO. 30

Date	Explanation	Post Ref.	Debit	Credit	Balance Debit	Balance Credit

LIPSTICK SALES   ACCOUNT NO. 40

Date	Explanation	Post Ref.	Debit	Credit	Balance Debit	Balance Credit

Name _____ Class _____ Date _____

PROBLEM 9A-4 OR PROBLEM 9B-4 (CONCLUDED)

SALES RETURNS & ALLOWANCES, LIPSTICK ACCOUNT NO. 42

Date	Explanation	Post Ref.	Debit	Credit	Balance Debit	Balance Credit

EYE SHADOW SALES ACCOUNT NO. 44

Date	Explanation	Post Ref.	Debit	Credit	Balance Debit	Balance Credit

(3)

BILL'S COSMETIC MARKET
SCHEDULE OF ACCOUNTS RECEIVABLE
APRIL 30, 200X

Name _____ Class _____ Date _____

CHAPTER 9
SUMMARY PRACTICE TEST
SALES AND CASH RECEIPTS

Part I Instructions

Fill in the blank(s) to complete the statement.

1. The normal balance of sales returns and allowances is _____.
2. _____ _____ and _____ is a contra-revenue account.
3. Sales is a(n) _____ account.
4. A discount period is less time than the _____ _____.
5. A debit to accounts receivable and a credit to sales records the sale of merchandise _____ _____.
6. The _____ _____ _____ _____ lists in alphabetical order an account for each customer.
7. _____ _____ in the general ledger is called the controlling account.
8. The (✓) in the PR column of the general journal indicates that the accounts receivable ledger has been updated _____ _____ _____.
9. Issuing _____ _____ results in a debit to sales returns and allowancs and a credit to accounts receivable.
10. In a wholesale company there is no _____ tax.
11. Sales Tax Payable is a(n) _____ in the general ledger.
12. Cash sales result in a(n) _____ to cash and a _____ to sales.
13. Sales Returns and Allowances is a(n) _____ _____ account.
14. The _____ _____ has to be posted to the general as well as the sales ledger.
15. No _____ _____ are taken on sales tax.
16. A(n) _____ _____ _____ _____ lists the ending balances from the accounts receivable ledger.

Part II

Complete the following chart:

Transaction	Dr.	Cr.
1. Sale for cash	_____	_____
2. Issued credit memo	_____	_____
3. Sale on account	_____	_____
4. Received cash payment less discount	_____	_____

Partial Chart of Accounts

10 Cash
20 Accounts Receivable

40 Sales
42 Sales Discount
44 Sales Returns and Allowances

Name _____ Class _____ Date _____

Part III Instructions

Answer true or false to the following statements.

1. A schedule of accounts receivable shows what customers do not owe.
2. A perpetual system would keep continual track of inventory.
3. Sales Discount policies can never change.
4. Sales Tax Payable is an asset.
5. Sales Discount is a contra asset.
6. Issuing a credit memorandum results in Sales, Returns and Allowances decreasing with Accounts Receivable increasing.
7. The sum of the accounts receivable subsidiary ledger is equal to the balance in the controlling account at the end of the month.
8. The buyer issues the credit memo.
9. The accounts receivable subsidiary ledger is listed in numerical order.
10. Sales Discount is a contra-revenue account.
11. Net sales = gross sales − SRA-SD.
12. The normal balance of an Accounts Receivable ledger is a debit.
13. Discounts are taken on sales tax.
14. 2/10, N/30 means a cash discount is good for 30 days.
15. The accounts receivable subsidiary ledger is always located in the general ledger.
16. Gross profit plus operating expenses equals net income.
17. A credit period is longer than the discount period.
18. In the accounts receivable subsidiary ledger each account is debited to record amounts customers owe.
19. Sales Tax Payable is an asset.

CHAPTER 9
SOLUTIONS TO SUMMARY PRACTICE TEST

Part I

1. debit
2. Sales Returns, Allowances
3. revenue
4. credit period
5. on account
6. accounts receivable subsidiary ledger
7. Accounts Receivable
8. during the month
9. credit memorandum
10. sales
11. liability
12. debit, credit
13. contra-revenue
14. journalized transaction
15. cash discounts
16. schedule of accounts receivable

SG-291

Part II

	Dr.	Cr.
1.	10	40
2.	44	20
3.	20	40
4.	10	20
	42	

Part III

1. false
2. true
3. false
4. false
5. false
6. false
7. true
8. false
9. false
10. true
11. true
12. true
13. false
14. false
15. false
16. false
17. true
18. true
19. false

CONTINUING PROBLEM FOR CHAPTER 9

SANCHEZ COMPUTER CENTER
GENERAL JOURNAL

PAGE 4

Date	Account Titles and Description	PR	Dr.	Cr.

Name _____ Class _____ Date _____

SANCHEZ COMPUTER CENTER
SCHEDULE OF ACCOUNTS RECEIVABLE
1/31/0X

_____
_____
_____
_____

CASH   **ACCOUNT NO. 1000**

Date	Explanation	Post Ref.	Debit	Credit	Balance Debit	Balance Credit
1/1 0X	Balance Forward	✓			3 336 65	

Name _____ Class _____ Date _____

SANCHEZ COMPUTER CENTER
PARTIAL GENERAL LEDGER

ACCOUNTS RECEIVABLE ACCOUNT NO. **1020**

Date		Explanation	Post Ref.	Debit	Credit	Balance Debit	Balance Credit
1/1	0X	Balance Forward	✔			13 600 00	

SALES ACCOUNT NO. **4010**

Date		Explanation	Post Ref.	Debit	Credit	Balance Debit	Balance Credit

SALES RETURNS & ALLOWANCES ACCOUNT NO. **4020**

Date		Explanation	Post Ref.	Debit	Credit	Balance Debit	Balance Credit

SALES DISCOUNTS   ACCOUNT NO. 4030

Date	Explanation	Post Ref.	Debit	Credit	Balance Debit	Balance Credit

ACCOUNTS RECEIVABLE SUBSIDIARY LEDGER

NAME TAYLOR GOLF   **ACCOUNT NO. 100**
ADDRESS 1010 MOCKINGBIRD LANE, CARLSBAD, CA 92008

Date	Explanation	Post Ref.	Debit	Credit	Dr. Balance
1/1 0X	Balance forward	✓			2,900.00

NAME VITA NEEDLE   **ACCOUNT NO. 101**
ADDRESS 144 CANTATA, IRVINE, CA 92606

Date	Explanation	Post Ref.	Debit	Credit	Dr. Balance
1/1 0X	Balance	✓			6,800.00

ACCOUNTS RECEIVABLE SUBSIDIARY LEDGER

NAME ACCU PAC   **ACCOUNT NO. 103**

ADDRESS 1717 JORDAN ST., SAN CLEMENTE, CA 91607

Date		Explanation	Post Ref.	Debit	Credit	Dr. Balance
1/1	0X	Balance	✓			3 9 0 0 00

NAME ANTHONY J. PITALE   **ACCOUNT NO. 104**

ADDRESS 600 NEWPORT BEACH, NEWPORT, CA 91600

Date		Explanation	Post Ref.	Debit	Credit	Dr. Balance

Purchases and Cash Payments

10

SELF-REVIEW QUIZ 10-1

1. _____ 2. _____ 3. _____ 4. _____ 5. _____

SELF-REVIEW QUIZ 10-2

MUNROE CO.
GENERAL JOURNAL

PAGE 1

Date	Account Titles and Description	PR	Dr.	Cr.

Name _____ Class _____ Date _____

ACCOUNTS PAYABLE SUBSIDIARY LEDGER

NAME JOHN BUTLER COMPANY

ADDRESS 18 REED RD., HOMEWOOD, IL 60430

Date	Explanation	Post Ref.	Debit	Credit	Cr. Balance

NAME FLYNN COMPANY

ADDRESS 15 FOSS AVE., ENGLEWOOD CLIFFS, NJ 07632

Date	Explanation	Post Ref.	Debit	Credit	Cr. Balance

PARTIAL GENERAL LEDGER

EQUIPMENT   **ACCOUNT NO. 121**

Date	Explanation	Post Ref.	Debit	Credit	Balance Debit	Balance Credit

Name _____ Class _____ Date _____

ACCOUNTS PAYABLE ACCOUNT NO. <u>212</u>

Date	Explanation	Post Ref.	Debit	Credit	Balance Debit	Balance Credit

PURCHASES ACCOUNT NO. <u>512</u>

Date	Explanation	Post Ref.	Debit	Credit	Balance Debit	Balance Credit

PURCHASES RETURNS AND ALLOWANCES ACCOUNT NO. <u>513</u>

Date	Explanation	Post Ref.	Debit	Credit	Balance Debit	Balance Credit

Name _____ Class _____ Date _____

SELF-REVIEW QUIZ 10-3

MELISSA COMPANY
GENERAL JOURNAL

PAGE 2

Date	Account Titles and Description	PR	Dr.	Cr.

ACCOUNTS PAYABLE SUBSIDARY LEDGER

NAME BOB FINKELSTEIN

ADDRESS 112 FLYING HIGHWAY, TRENTON, NJ 00861

Date 200X	Explanation	Post Ref.	Debit	Credit	Cr. Balance
June 1	Balance	✔			300 00

NAME AL JEEP

ADDRESS 118 WANG RD., SAUGUS, MA 01432

Date 200X	Explanation	Post Ref.	Debit	Credit	Cr. Balance
June 1	Balance	✔			200 00

PARTIAL GENERAL LEDGER

CASH   ACCOUNT NO. <u>110</u>

Date 200X		Explanation	Post Ref.	Debit	Credit	Balance Debit	Balance Credit
June	1	Balance	✓			700 00	

ACCOUNTS PAYABLE   ACCOUNT NO. <u>210</u>

Date 200X		Explanation	Post Ref.	Debit	Credit	Balance Debit	Balance Credit
June	1	Balance	✓				500 00

PURCHASES DISCOUNT   ACCOUNT NO. <u>511</u>

Date		Explanation	Post Ref.	Debit	Credit	Balance Debit	Balance Credit

ADVERTISING EXPENSE   ACCOUNT NO. <u>610</u>

Date		Explanation	Post Ref.	Debit	Credit	Balance Debit	Balance Credit

SELF-REVIEW QUIZ 10-4

PETE'S CLOCK SHOP
GENERAL JOURNAL

PAGE 2

Date	Account Titles and Description	PR	Dr.	Cr.

PETE'S CLOCK SHOP
GENERAL JOURNAL

PAGE 3

Date	Account Titles and Description	PR	Dr.	Cr.

Name _____ Class _____ Date _____

CHAPTER 10
FORMS FOR CLASSROOM DEMONSTRATION EXERCISES SET A OR SET B

1. A. _____ D. _____
   B. _____ E. _____
   C. _____ F. _____

2.

3. _____
   _____
   _____
   _____
   _____
   _____
   _____
   _____
   _____

4. A. _____
   B. _____
   C. _____

5.

SG-306

6.

WEB.COM
SCHEDULE OF ACCOUNTS PAYABLE
MAY 31, 200X

7.

FORM FOR CLASSROOM DEMONSTRATION EXERCISES 8, 9, 10

Date	Account Titles and Description	PR	Dr.	Cr.

FORMS FOR EXERCISES

10-1.

Lee's.com	Equipment 120

Lane.com	Accounts Payable 210

Sail.com	Purchases 510

10-2. PAGE 1

Reel Co.	Accounts Payable 211	Purchases Returns and Allowances 513

EXERCISES (CONTINUED)

10-3. PAGE 2

Date	Account Titles and Description	PR	Dr.	Cr.

ACCOUNTS PAYABLE SUBSIDIARY LEDGER

A. James
| | 1,000 |

B. Foss
| | 400 |

J. Ranch
| | 900 |

B. Swanson
| | 100 |

PARTIAL GENERAL LEDGER

Cash 110
| 3,000 | |

Accounts Payable 210
| | 2,400 |

Purchases Discount 511

Advertising Expense 610

EXERCISES (CONTINUED)

10-4.

MORGAN'S CLOTHING
SCHEDULE OF ACCOUNTS PAYABLE
APRIL 30, 200X

_____
_____
_____
_____

       Accounts Payable   210
_____|_____

10-5.

Accounts Affected	Category	↑↓	Rules

10-6.

_____
_____
_____
_____
_____

Name _____ Class _____ Date _____

FORM FOR EXERCISES 10-7, 10-8, 10-9, 10-10

Date	Account Titles and Description	PR	Dr.	Cr.

Name _____ Class _____ Date _____

FORM FOR EXERCISES 10-7, 10-8, 10-9, 10-10 (CONTINUED)

Date	Account Titles and Description	PR	Dr.	Cr.

CALCULATIONS PAGE FOR 10-7 TO 10-10

END OF CHAPTER PROBLEMS

PROBLEM 10A-1 OR PROBLEM 10B-1

RON'S SKATE SHOP
GENERAL JOURNAL

PAGE 2

Date	Account Titles and Description	PR	Dr.	Cr.

PROBLEM 10A-1 OR PROBLEM 10B-1 (CONTINUED)

ACCOUNTS PAYABLE SUBSIDIARY LEDGER

NAME MAIL.COM

ADDRESS 12 SMITH ST., DEARBORN, MI 09113

Date	Explanation	Post Ref.	Debit	Credit	Cr. Balance

NAME NORTON CO.

ADDRESS 1 RANTOUL RD., CHARLOTTE, NC 01114

Date	Explanation	Post Ref.	Debit	Credit	Cr. Balance

NAME ROLO CO.

ADDRESS 2 WEST RD., LYNN, MA 01471

Date	Explanation	Post Ref.	Debit	Credit	Cr. Balance

PARTIAL GENERAL LEDGER

STORE SUPPLIES   **ACCOUNT NO. 115**

Date	Explanation	Post Ref.	Debit	Credit	Balance Debit	Balance Credit

PROBLEM 10A-1 OR PROBLEM 10B-1 (CONCLUDED)

STORE EQUIPMENT   **ACCOUNT NO. 121**

Date	Explanation	Post Ref.	Debit	Credit	Balance Debit	Balance Credit

ACCOUNTS PAYABLE   **ACCOUNT NO. 210**

Date	Explanation	Post Ref.	Debit	Credit	Balance Debit	Balance Credit

PURCHASES   **ACCOUNT NO. 510**

Date	Explanation	Post Ref.	Debit	Credit	Balance Debit	Balance Credit

Name _____ Class _____ Date _____

PROBLEM 10A-2 OR PROBLEM 10B-2

MABEL'S NATURAL FOOD

PAGE 2

Date	Account Titles and Description	PR	Dr.	Cr.

PROBLEM 10A-2 OR PROBLEM 10B-2 (CONTINUED)

ACCOUNTS PAYABLE SUBSIDIARY LEDGER

NAME ATON CO.

ADDRESS 11 LYNNWAY AVE., NEWPORT, RI 03112

Date 200X	Explanation	Post Ref.	Debit	Credit	Cr. Balance
May 1	Balance	✓			400 00

NAME BROWARD CO.

ADDRESS 21 RIVER ST., ANAHEIM, CA 43110

Date 200X	Explanation	Post Ref.	Debit	Credit	Cr. Balance
May 1	Balance	✓			600 00

NAME MIDDEN CO.

ADDRESS 10 ASTER RD., DUBUQUE, IA 80021

Date 200X	Explanation	Post Ref.	Debit	Credit	Cr. Balance
May 1	Balance	✓			1 200 00

NAME RELAR CO.

ADDRESS 22 GERALD RD., SMITH, CO 43138

Date 200X	Explanation	Post Ref.	Debit	Credit	Cr. Balance
May 1	Balance	✓			500 00

PROBLEM 10A-2 OR PROBLEM 10B-2 (CONTINUED)

PARTIAL GENERAL LEDGER

STORE SUPPLIES — ACCOUNT NO. 110

Date	Explanation	Post Ref.	Debit	Credit	Balance Debit	Balance Credit

OFFICE EQUIPMENT — ACCOUNT NO. 120

Date	Explanation	Post Ref.	Debit	Credit	Balance Debit	Balance Credit

ACCOUNTS PAYABLE — ACCOUNT NO. 210

Date 200X	Explanation	Post Ref.	Debit	Credit	Balance Debit	Balance Credit
May 1	Balance	✓				2 700 00

PURCHASES — ACCOUNT NO. 510

Date 200X	Explanation	Post Ref.	Debit	Credit	Balance Debit	Balance Credit
May 1	Balance	✓			16 000 00	

PROBLEM 10A-2 OR PROBLEM 10B-2 (CONCLUDED)

PURCHASES RETURNS AND ALLOWANCES **ACCOUNT NO. 512**

Date	Explanation	Post Ref.	Debit	Credit	Balance Debit	Balance Credit

MABEL'S NATURAL FOOD

SCHEDULE OF ACCOUNTS PAYABLE

MAY 31, 200X

Name _____ Class _____ Date _____

PROBLEM 10A-3 OR PROBLEM 10B-3

PAGE 5

Date	Account Titles and Description	PR	Dr.	Cr.

PROBLEM 10A-3 OR PROBLEM 10B-3 (CONTINUED)

ACCOUNTS PAYABLE SUBSIDIARY LEDGER

NAME ALVIN CO.

ADDRESS 1 REACH RD., IPSWICH, MA 01932

Date 200X		Explanation	Post Ref.	Debit	Credit	Cr. Balance
May	1	Balance	✔			1 2 0 0 00

NAME HENRY CO.

ADDRESS 1 RALPH RD., REVERE, MA 01321

Date 200X		Explanation	Post Ref.	Debit	Credit	Cr. Balance
May	1	Balance	✔			6 0 0 00

NAME SOY CO.

ADDRESS 7 PLYMOUTH AVE., GLENN, NH 01218

Date 200X		Explanation	Post Ref.	Debit	Credit	Cr. Balance
May	1	Balance	✔			8 0 0 00

NAME XON CO.

ADDRESS 22 REY RD., BOCA RATON, FL 99132

Date 200X		Explanation	Post Ref.	Debit	Credit	Cr. Balance
May	1	Balance	✔			1 4 0 0 00

PROBLEM 10A-3 OR PROBLEM 10B-3 (CONTINUED)

PARTIAL GENERAL LEDGER

CASH   ACCOUNT NO. 110

Date 200X	Explanation	Post Ref.	Debit	Credit	Balance Debit	Balance Credit
May 1	Balance	✔			17 000 00	

DELIVERY TRUCK   ACCOUNT NO. 150

Date 200X	Explanation	Post Ref.	Debit	Credit	Balance Debit	Balance Credit

ACCOUNTS PAYABLE   ACCOUNT NO. 210

Date 200X	Explanation	Post Ref.	Debit	Credit	Balance Debit	Balance Credit
May 1	Balance	✔				4 000 00

COMPUTER PURCHASES   ACCOUNT NO. 510

Date 200X	Explanation	Post Ref.	Debit	Credit	Balance Debit	Balance Credit

Name _____ Class _____ Date _____

PROBLEM 10A-3 OR PROBLEM 10B-3 (CONCLUDED)

COMPUTER PURCHASES DISCOUNT   ACCOUNT NO. <u>511</u>

Date	Explanation	Post Ref.	Debit	Credit	Balance Debit	Balance Credit

RENT EXPENSE   ACCOUNT NO. <u>610</u>

Date	Explanation	Post Ref.	Debit	Credit	Balance Debit	Balance Credit

UTILITIES EXPENSE   ACCOUNT NO. <u>620</u>

Date	Explanation	Post Ref.	Debit	Credit	Balance Debit	Balance Credit

JONES COMPUTER CENTER
SCHEDULE OF ACCOUNTS PAYABLE
MAY 31, 200X

PROBLEM 10A-4 OR PROBLEM 10B-4

(1)

ABBY'S TOY HOUSE
GENERAL JOURNAL

PAGE 1

Date	Account Titles and Description	PR	Dr.	Cr.

PROBLEM 10A-4 OR PROBLEM 10B-4 (CONTINUED)

PAGE 2

Date	Account Titles and Description	PR	Dr.	Cr.

Name _____ Class _____ Date _____

PROBLEM 10A-4 OR PROBLEM 10B-4 (CONTINUED)

PAGE 3

Date	Account Titles and Description	PR	Dr.	Cr.

PROBLEM 10A-4 OR PROBLEM 10B-4 (CONTINUED)

PAGE 4

Date	Account Titles and Description	PR	Dr.	Cr.

Name _____ Class _____ Date _____

PROBLEM 10A-4 OR PROBLEM 10B-4 (CONTINUED)

PAGE 5

Date	Account Titles and Description	PR	Dr.	Cr.

SG-328

Name _____ Class _____ Date _____

PROBLEM 10A-4 OR PROBLEM 10B-4 (CONTINUED)

(2)   ACCOUNTS PAYABLE SUBSIDIARY LEDGER

NAME   MINNIE KATZ
ADDRESS   87 GARFIELD AVE., REVERE, MA 01245

Date	Explanation	Post Ref.	Debit	Credit	Cr. Balance

NAME   SAM KATZ GARAGE
ADDRESS   22 REGIS RD., BOSTON, MA 01950

Date	Explanation	Post Ref.	Debit	Credit	Cr. Balance

NAME   EARL MILLER CO.
ADDRESS   22 RETTER ST., SAN DIEGO, CA 01211

Date	Explanation	Post Ref.	Debit	Credit	Cr. Balance

NAME   WOODY SMITH
ADDRESS   2 SPRING ST., WEERS, ND 02118

Date	Explanation	Post Ref.	Debit	Credit	Cr. Balance

Name _____ Class _____ Date _____

PROBLEM 10A-4 OR PROBLEM 10B-4 (CONTINUED)

ACCOUNTS RECEIVABLE SUBSIDIARY LEDGER

NAME BILL BURTON

ADDRESS 24 RYAN RD., BUIKE, OH 02183

Date	Explanation	Post Ref.	Debit	Credit	Dr. Balance

NAME BONNIE FLOW CO.

ADDRESS 2 SMITH RD., DALLAS, TX 22210

Date	Explanation	Post Ref.	Debit	Credit	Dr. Balance

NAME JIM REX

ADDRESS 1 SCHOOL ST., CLEVELAND, OH 22441

Date	Explanation	Post Ref.	Debit	Credit	Dr. Balance

PROBLEM 10A-4 OR PROBLEM 10B-4 (CONTINUED)

NAME   AMY ROSE

ADDRESS   18 VEEK RD., CHESTER, CT 80111

Date	Explanation	Post Ref.	Debit	Credit	Dr. Balance

GENERAL LEDGER

CASH   **ACCOUNT NO. 110**

Date	Explanation	Post Ref.	Debit	Credit	Balance Debit	Balance Credit

PROBLEM 10A-4 OR PROBLEM 10B-4 (CONTINUED)

ACCOUNTS RECEIVABLE — ACCOUNT NO. 112

Date	Explanation	Post Ref.	Debit	Credit	Balance Debit	Balance Credit

PREPAID RENT — ACCOUNT NO. 114

Date	Explanation	Post Ref.	Debit	Credit	Balance Debit	Balance Credit

DELIVERY TRUCK — ACCOUNT NO. 121

Date	Explanation	Post Ref.	Debit	Credit	Balance Debit	Balance Credit

PROBLEM 10A-4 OR PROBLEM 10B-4 (CONTINUED)

ACCOUNTS PAYABLE　　　　　　　　　　　　ACCOUNT NO. 210

Date	Explanation	Post Ref.	Debit	Credit	Balance Debit	Balance Credit

A. ELLEN, CAPITAL　　　　　　　　　　　　ACCOUNT NO. 310

Date	Explanation	Post Ref.	Debit	Credit	Balance Debit	Balance Credit

TOY SALES　　　　　　　　　　　　　　　　ACCOUNT NO. 410

Date	Explanation	Post Ref.	Debit	Credit	Balance Debit	Balance Credit

PROBLEM 10A-4 OR PROBLEM 10B-4 (CONTINUED)

SALES RETURNS AND ALLOWANCES   ACCOUNT NO. 412

Date	Explanation	Post Ref.	Debit	Credit	Balance Debit	Balance Credit

SALES DISCOUNTS   ACCOUNT NO. 414

Date	Explanation	Post Ref.	Debit	Credit	Balance Debit	Balance Credit

TOY PURCHASES   ACCOUNT NO. 510

Date	Explanation	Post Ref.	Debit	Credit	Balance Debit	Balance Credit

PURCHASES RETURNS AND ALLOWANCES   ACCOUNT NO. 512

Date	Explanation	Post Ref.	Debit	Credit	Balance Debit	Balance Credit

PROBLEM 10A-4 OR PROBLEM 10B-4 (CONTINUED)

PURCHASES DISCOUNT   ACCOUNT NO. 514

Date	Explanation	Post Ref.	Debit	Credit	Balance Debit	Balance Credit

SALARIES EXPENSE   ACCOUNT NO. 610

Date	Explanation	Post Ref.	Debit	Credit	Balance Debit	Balance Credit

CLEANING EXPENSE   ACCOUNT NO. 612

Date	Explanation	Post Ref.	Debit	Credit	Balance Debit	Balance Credit

PROBLEM 10A-4 OR PROBLEM 10B-4 (CONCLUDED)

(3)

ABBY'S TOY HOUSE
SCHEDULE OF ACCOUNTS RECEIVABLE
MARCH 31, 200X

(3)

ABBY'S TOY HOUSE
SCHEDULE OF ACCOUNTS PAYABLE
MARCH 31, 200X

PROBLEM 10A-5 OR PROBLEM 10B-5

PAGE 3

Date	Account Titles and Description	PR	Dr.	Cr.

PROBLEM 10A-5 OR PROBLEM 10B-5 (CONCLUDED)

PAGE 4

Date	Account Titles and Description	PR	Dr.	Cr.

CHAPTER 10
SUMMARY PRACTICE TEST
PURCHASES AND CASH PAYMENTS

Part I Instructions

Fill in the blank(s) to complete the statement.

1. The trend in accounting is more to _____ inventory rather than _____ inventory.

2. Purchase discounts are categorized as a(n) _____ _____ account.

3. The Purchases account has a _____ balance.

4. Purchases are defined as merchandise for _____ to customers.

5. The accounts payable subsidiary ledger represents a potential _____ of cash.

6. The controlling account in the general ledger for the accounts payable subsidiary ledger is called _____ _____.

7. The accounts payable subsidiary ledger would be recorded _____.

8. The balance in the Accounts Payable controlling account should be equal to the sum of the accounts payable subsidiary ledger accounts _____ _____ _____ _____.

9. In perpetual inventory, purchases are recorded as _____ _____.

10. The ✔ in the reference column indicates that the _____ _____ _____ _____ has been updated.

11. A(n) _____ _____ that is issued means the buyer owes less money, as merchandise is being returned or an allowance received.

12. A debit memorandum issued or a credit memorandum received results in a(n) _____ to Accounts Payable and a credit to Purchases, Returns and Allowances.

13. List price − net price = _____ _____ amount.

14. The accounts payable subsidiary ledger is listed in _____ _____.

15. Purchases Returns and Allowances is increased by a(n) _____.

16. Cost of goods sold is classified as a(n) _____.

17. In a perpetual inventory system, freight is recorded in the _____ _____ account.

18. Purchases Discounts is increased by _____.

19. A(n) _____ _____ provides the purchasing department the information to then prepare a purchase order.

20. A(n) _____ _____ is made out after a company inspects received shipments.

Name _____ Class _____ Date _____

Part II

Complete the following table:

	Account Title	CAT	↑↓	Financial Statement
1.	Purchases			
2.	Purchase Discount			
3.	Accounts Receivable			
4.	Cost of Goods Sold			
5.	Salary Expenses			
6.	Accounts Payable			
7.	Purchase Returns and Allowances			
8.	Cash			
9.	Supplies			
10.	Sale Discount			

Part III Instructions

Answer true or false to the following statements.

1. F.O.B. shipping point means the seller is responsible to cover shipping costs.
2. The Purchases account is a contra-cost of goods sold account.
3. Purchases discounts are the result of paying for equipment within the discount period.
4. F.O.B. Destination means the seller is responsible to cover shipping costs.
5. Purchases discounts are taken on freight.
6. Merchandise inventory is an asset.
7. Cost of goods sold is a cost.
8. The balance in Accounts Payable, the controlling account, will be equal to the sum of the accounts receivable subsidiary ledger at the end of the month.
9. A purchase order is completed after the purchase requisition.
10. On receiving a purchase order, the seller may issue a sales invoice.
11. The normal balance of Purchases Discount is a debit balance.
12. The seller will often issue a debit memorandum to the buyer.
13. Cost of goods sold is used in a periodic inventory system.
14. Returned equipment by a buyer results in a change in Purchases Returns and Allowances.
15. Trade discounts do not occur because of early payments of one's bills.
16. A seller's sales discount on purchases is the buyer's purchases discount.
17. Buying of equipment on account is only recorded in the general ledger.
18. On receiving a debit memorandum, the seller will issue a credit memorandum.
19. Returns in a perpetual accounting system are recorded in the merchandise inventory account.
20. Purchases are contra costs.

CHAPTER 10
SOLUTIONS TO SUMMARY PRACTICE TEST

Part I

1. perpetual, periodic
2. contra-cost
3. debit
4. resale
5. outflow
6. accounts payable
7. daily
8. at end of month
9. merchandise inventory
10. accounts payable subsidiary ledger
11. debit memorandum
12. debit
13. trade discount
14. alphabetical order
15. credit
16. cost
17. merchandise inventory
18. credits
19. purchase requisition
20. receiving report

Part II

1. cost — Dr — Cr — Income Statement
2. contra-cost — Cr — Dr — Income Statement
3. asset — Dr — Cr — Balance Sheet
4. cost — Dr — Cr — Income Statement
5. expense — Dr — Cr — Income Statement
6. liability — Cr — Dr — Balance Sheet
7. contra-cost — Cr — Dr — Income Statement
8. asset — Dr — Cr — Balance Sheet
9. asset — Dr — Cr — Balance Sheet
10. contra-revenue — Dr — Cr — Income Statement

Part III

1. false
2. false
3. true
4. true
5. false
6. true
7. true
8. false
9. true
10. true
11. false
12. false
13. false
14. true
15. true
16. true
17. false
18. true
19. true
20. false

CONTINUING PROBLEM FOR CHAPTER 10

SANCHEZ COMPUTER CENTER
GENERAL JOURNAL

PAGE 5

Date	Account Titles and Description	PR	Dr.	Cr.

Name _____ Class _____ Date _____

PARTIAL GENERAL LEDGER

CASH   ACCOUNT NO. 1000

Date		Explanation	Post Ref.	Debit	Credit	Balance Debit	Balance Credit
2/1	0X	Balance forward	✔			15 1 1 6 65	

SUPPLIES   ACCOUNT NO. 1030

Date		Explanation	Post Ref.	Debit	Credit	Balance Debit	Balance Credit
2/1	0X	Balance forward	✔			1 3 2 00	

MERCHANDISE INVENTORY   ACCOUNT NO. 1040

Date	Explanation	Post Ref.	Debit	Credit	Balance Debit	Balance Credit

Name _____ Class _____ Date _____

PREPAID RENT — ACCOUNT NO. 1025

Date	Explanation	Post Ref.	Debit	Credit	Balance Debit	Balance Credit
2/1 0X	Balance forward	✔			1 600 00	

ACCOUNTS PAYABLE — ACCOUNT NO. 2000

Date	Explanation	Post Ref.	Debit	Credit	Balance Debit	Balance Credit
2/1 0X	Balance forward	✔				2 050 00

PURCHASES — ACCOUNT NO. 6000

Date	Explanation	Post Ref.	Debit	Credit	Balance Debit	Balance Credit

PURCHASE RETURNS AND ALLOWANCES — ACCOUNT NO. 6010

Date	Explanation	Post Ref.	Debit	Credit	Balance Debit	Balance Credit

PURCHASE DISCOUNTS — ACCOUNT NO. 6020

Date	Explanation	Post Ref.	Debit	Credit	Balance Debit	Balance Credit

SANCHEZ COMPUTER CENTER
SCHEDULE OF ACCOUNTS PAYABLE
2/28/0X

ACCOUNTS PAYABLE SUBSIDIARY LEDGER

NAME MULTI SYSTEMS, INC. # 6A3
ADDRESS 1919 MORAN ST., ANAHEIM, CA 92606

Date		Explanation	Post Ref.	Debit	Credit	Cr. Balance
2/1	0X	Balance forward	✔			450 00

NAME OFFICE DEPOT # 6A4
ADDRESS 460 ESCONDIDO BLVD., ESCONDIDO, CA 92025

Date		Explanation	Post Ref.	Debit	Credit	Cr. Balance
2/1	0X	Balance forward	✔			50 00

NAME SAN DIEGO ELECTRIC   # 6A5
ADDRESS 606 INDUSTRIAL ST., SAN DIEGO, CA 92121

Date	Explanation	Post Ref.	Debit	Credit	Cr. Balance

NAME PAC BELL   # 6A6
ADDRESS 101 BELL AVE., SAN DIEGO, CA 92101

Date	Explanation	Post Ref.	Debit	Credit	Cr. Balance
2/1 0X	Balance forward	✔			1 5 0 00

NAME COMPUTER CONNECTION   # 6A7
ADDRESS 1020 WIL LANE, LOS ANGELES, CA 92405

Date	Explanation	Post Ref.	Debit	Credit	Cr. Balance

Name _____ Class _____ Date _____

NAME	SYSTEM DESIGN FURNITURE	# 6A8
ADDRESS	2070 FIRST ST., SAN DIEGO, CA 92101	

Date		Explanation	Post Ref.	Debit	Credit	Cr. Balance
2/1	0X	Balance forward	✔			1 4 0 0 00

SG-348

Name _____ Class _____ Date _____

APPENDIX 10A
FORMS FOR CLASSROOM DEMONSTRATION PROBLEM — SPECIAL JOURNALS

J. LING CO.
SALES JOURNAL

PAGE 1

Date	Account Debited	Terms	Invoice No.	Post Ref.	Dr. Acc. Receivable Cr. Sales

CASH RECEIPTS JOURNAL

PAGE 1

Date	Cash Dr.	Sales Discounts Dr.	Accounts Receivable Cr.	Sales Cr.	Sundry Account Name	PR	Amount Cr.

PURCHASES JOURNAL

PAGE 1

Date	Account Credited	Terms	PR	Accounts Payable Cr.	Purchases Dr.	Sundry Dr. Account	PR	Amount

CASH PAYMENTS JOURNAL

PAGE 1

Date	Check No.	Accounts Debited	PR	Sundry Account Dr.	Accounts Payable Dr.	Purchases Discounts Cr.	Cash Cr.

Name _____ Class _____ Date _____

DEMONSTRATION PROBLEM (CONTINUED)

GENERAL JOURNAL

PAGE 1

Date	Account Titles and Description	PR	Dr.	Cr.

ACCOUNTS RECEIVABLE SUBSIDIARY LEDGER

NAME BALDER CO.

ADDRESS 1 ROCK RD., DENVER, CO 66083

Date	Explanation	Post Ref.	Debit	Credit	Dr. Balance

NAME LEWIS CO.

ADDRESS 15 SMITH AVE., REVERE, MA 01545

Date	Explanation	Post Ref.	Debit	Credit	Dr. Balance

DEMONSTRATION PROBLEM (CONCLUDED)

ACCOUNTS PAYABLE SUBSIDIARY LEDGER

NAME CASE CO.

ADDRESS 1 LONG RD., MARLBOROUGH, MA 01545

Date	Explanation	Post Ref.	Debit	Credit	Cr. Balance

NAME NOONE CO.

ADDRESS 11 MILL RD., MALDEN, OK 01143

Date	Explanation	Post Ref.	Debit	Credit	Cr. Balance

PARTIAL GENERAL LEDGER

Cash 111

Accounts Receivable 112

Equipment 116

Accounts Payable 210

J. Ling, Capital 310

Sales 410

Sales Returns & Allowances 420

Sales Discount 430

Purchases 510

Purchases Returns & Allowances 520

Purchases Discounts 530

Salaries Expense 610

CHAPTER 10A APPENDIX FORMS

PROBLEM A-1

(1, 2)

FOOD.COM
SALES JOURNAL

PAGE 1

Date	Account Debited	Invoice No.	PR	Accounts Receivable Dr.	Pizza Sales Cr.	Grocery Sales Cr.

(1, 2)

FOOD.COM
GENERAL JOURNAL

PAGE 1

Date	Account Titles and Description	PR	Dr.	Cr.

Name _____ Class _____ Date _____

PROBLEM A-1 (CONTINUED)

ACCOUNTS RECEIVABLE SUBSIDIARY LEDGER

NAME DUNCAN CO.

ADDRESS 942 MOSE ST., REVERE, MA 01938

Date	Explanation	Post Ref.	Debit	Credit	Dr. Balance

NAME LONG CO.

ADDRESS 8 JOSS AVE., LYNN, MA 01947

Date	Explanation	Post Ref.	Debit	Credit	Dr. Balance

NAME SUE MOORE CO.

ADDRESS 10 LOST RD., TOPSFIELD, MA 01998

Date	Explanation	Post Ref.	Debit	Credit	Dr. Balance

PROBLEM A-1 (CONTINUED)

FOOD.COM
GENERAL LEDGER

ACCOUNTS RECEIVABLE   ACCOUNT NO. <u>112</u>

Date	Explanation	Post Ref.	Debit	Credit	Balance Debit	Balance Credit

PIZZA SALES   ACCOUNT NO. <u>410</u>

Date	Explanation	Post Ref.	Debit	Credit	Balance Debit	Balance Credit

GROCERY SALES   ACCOUNT NO. <u>411</u>

Date	Explanation	Post Ref.	Debit	Credit	Balance Debit	Balance Credit

SALES RETURNS AND ALLOWANCES   ACCOUNT NO. <u>412</u>

Date	Explanation	Post Ref.	Debit	Credit	Balance Debit	Balance Credit

Name _____ Class _____ Date _____

PROBLEM A-1 (CONCLUDED)

FOOD.COM
SCHEDULE OF ACCOUNTS RECEIVABLE
JUNE 30, 200X

PROBLEM A-2

(1, 2)

TED'S AUTO SUPPLY
SALES JOURNAL

PAGE 4

Date	Customer's Name Account Receivable	Invoice No.	PR	Accounts Receivable Dr.	Sales Tax Payable Cr.	Auto Parts Sales Cr.

PROBLEM A-2 (CONTINUED)

(1, 2)

TED'S AUTO SUPPLY
GENERAL JOURNAL

PAGE 2

Date	Account Titles and Description	PR	Dr.	Cr.

PROBLEM A-2 (CONTINUED)

ACCOUNTS RECEIVABLE SUBSIDIARY LEDGER

NAME   LANCE CORNER
ADDRESS   9 ROE ST., BARTLETT, NH 01382

Date 200X		Explanation	Post Ref.	Debit	Credit	Dr. Balance
Nov	1	Balance	✔			400 00

NAME   J. SETH
ADDRESS   22 REESE ST., LACONIA, NH 04321

Date 200X		Explanation	Post Ref.	Debit	Credit	Dr. Balance
Nov	1	Balance	✔			200 00

NAME   R. VOLAN
ADDRESS   12 ASTER RD., MERRIMACK, NH 02134

Date 200X		Explanation	Post Ref.	Debit	Credit	Dr. Balance
Nov	1	Balance	✔			1000 00

PROBLEM A-2 (CONTINUED)

TED'S AUTO SUPPLY
GENERAL JOURNAL

ACCOUNTS RECEIVABLE — ACCOUNT NO. 110

Date 200X		Explanation	Post Ref.	Debit	Credit	Balance Debit	Balance Credit
Nov	1	Balance	✔			1 600 00	

SALES TAX PAYABLE — ACCOUNT NO. 210

Date 200X		Explanation	Post Ref.	Debit	Credit	Balance Debit	Balance Credit
Nov	1	Balance	✔				1 600 00

AUTO PARTS SALES — ACCOUNT NO. 410

Date	Explanation	Post Ref.	Debit	Credit	Balance Debit	Balance Credit

SALES RETURNS AND ALLOWANCES — ACCOUNT NO. 420

Date	Explanation	Post Ref.	Debit	Credit	Balance Debit	Balance Credit

PROBLEM A-2 (CONCLUDED)

(3)

TED'S AUTO SUPPLY
SCHEDULE OF ACCOUNTS RECEIVABLE
NOVEMBER 30, 200X

PROBLEM A-3

SKATES.COM
PURCHASES JOURNAL
PAGE 3

Date	Account Credited	Date of Invoice	Inv. No.	Terms	PR	Accounts Payable Cr.	Purchases Dr.	Sundry Dr.		
								Account	PR	Amount

PROBLEM A-3 (CONTINUED)

ACCOUNTS PAYABLE SUBSIDIARY LEDGER

NAME MAIL.COM

ADDRESS 12 SMITH ST., DEARBORN, MI 09113

Date	Explanation	Post Ref.	Debit	Credit	Cr. Balance

NAME NORTON CO.

ADDRESS 1 RANTOUL RD., CHARLOTTE, NC 01114

Date	Explanation	Post Ref.	Debit	Credit	Cr. Balance

NAME ROLO CO.

ADDRESS 2 WEST RD., LYNN, MA 01471

Date	Explanation	Post Ref.	Debit	Credit	Cr. Balance

PARTIAL GENERAL LEDGER

STORE SUPPLIES   **ACCOUNT NO. 115**

Date	Explanation	Post Ref.	Debit	Credit	Balance Debit	Balance Credit

PROBLEM A-3 (CONCLUDED)

STORE EQUIPMENT   **ACCOUNT NO. 121**

Date	Explanation	Post Ref.	Debit	Credit	Balance Debit	Balance Credit

ACCOUNTS PAYABLE   **ACCOUNT NO. 210**

Date	Explanation	Post Ref.	Debit	Credit	Balance Debit	Balance Credit

PURCHASES   **ACCOUNT NO. 510**

Date	Explanation	Post Ref.	Debit	Credit	Balance Debit	Balance Credit

PROBLEM A-4

**MABEL'S NATURAL FOOD STORE
PURCHASES JOURNAL**

PAGE 10

Date	Account Credited	Date of Invoice	Inv. No.	Terms	PR	Accounts Payable Cr.	Purchases Dr.	Store Supplies Dr.	Sundry Dr.		
									Account	PR	Amount

PROBLEM A-4 (CONTINUED)

ACCOUNTS PAYABLE SUBSIDIARY LEDGER

NAME ATON CO.

ADDRESS 11 LYNNWAY AVE., NEWPORT, RI 03112

Date 200X		Explanation	Post Ref.	Debit	Credit	Cr. Balance
May	1	Balance	✓			400 00

NAME BROWARD CO.

ADDRESS 21 RIVER ST., ANAHEIM, CA 43110

Date 200X		Explanation	Post Ref.	Debit	Credit	Cr. Balance
May	1	Balance	✓			600 00

NAME MIDDEN CO.

ADDRESS 10 ASTER RD., DUBUQUE, IA 80021

Date 200X		Explanation	Post Ref.	Debit	Credit	Cr. Balance
May	1	Balance	✓			1 200 00

NAME RELAR CO.

ADDRESS 22 GERALD RD., SMITH, CO 43138

Date 200X		Explanation	Post Ref.	Debit	Credit	Cr. Balance
May	1	Balance	✓			500 00

PROBLEM A-4 (CONTINUED)

PARTIAL GENERAL LEDGER

STORE SUPPLIES — ACCOUNT NO. 110

Date	Explanation	Post Ref.	Debit	Credit	Balance Debit	Balance Credit

OFFICE EQUIPMENT — ACCOUNT NO. 120

Date	Explanation	Post Ref.	Debit	Credit	Balance Debit	Balance Credit

ACCOUNTS PAYABLE — ACCOUNT NO. 210

Date 200X	Explanation	Post Ref.	Debit	Credit	Balance Debit	Balance Credit
May 1	Balance	✔				2 700 00

PURCHASES — ACCOUNT NO. 510

Date 200X	Explanation	Post Ref.	Debit	Credit	Balance Debit	Balance Credit
May 1	Balance	✔			16 700 00	

PROBLEM A-4 (CONCLUDED)

PURCHASES RETURNS AND ALLOWANCES   **ACCOUNT NO. 512**

Date	Explanation	Post Ref.	Debit	Credit	Balance Debit	Balance Credit

GENERAL JOURNAL   PAGE 2

Date	Account Titles and Description	PR	Dr.	Cr.

MABEL'S NATURAL FOOD STORE
SCHEDULE OF ACCOUNTS PAYABLE
MAY 31, 200X

PROBLEM A-5

(1, 3)

ABBY'S TOY HOUSE
PURCHASES JOURNAL

PAGE 1

Date	Account Credited	Date of Inv.	Inv. No.	Terms	PR	Accounts Payable Cr.	Toy Purchases Dr.	Sundry Dr.		
								Accounts	PR	Amount

PROBLEM A-5 (CONTINUED)

ABBY'S TOY HOUSE
CASH RECEIPTS JOURNAL
PAGE 1

Date	Cash Dr.	Sales Discounts Dr.	Accounts Receivable Cr.	Toy Sales Cr.	Sundry Account	PR	Amount Cr.

PROBLEM A-5 (CONTINUED)

ABBY'S TOY HOUSE
CASH PAYMENTS JOURNAL

PAGE 1

Date	Check No.	Account Debited	PR	Sundry Dr.	Accounts Payable Dr.	Purchases Discount Cr.	Cash Cr.

PROBLEM A-5 (CONTINUED)

**ABBY'S TOY HOUSE
SALES JOURNAL
MARCH 31, 200X**

PAGE 1

Date	Account Debited	Invoice No.	Terms	PR	Accounts Rec. – Dr. Toy Sales – Cr.

**ABBY'S TOY HOUSE
GENERAL JOURNAL
MARCH 31, 200X**

PAGE 1

Date	Account Titles and Description	PR	Dr.	Cr.

Name _____ Class _____ Date _____

PROBLEM A-5 (CONTINUED)

(2)   **ACCOUNTS PAYABLE SUBSIDIARY LEDGER**

NAME   MINNIE KATZ
ADDRESS   87 GARFIELD AVE., REVERE, MA 01245

Date	Explanation	Post Ref.	Debit	Credit	Cr. Balance

NAME   SAM KATZ GARAGE
ADDRESS   22 REGIS RD., BOSTON, MA 01950

Date	Explanation	Post Ref.	Debit	Credit	Cr. Balance

NAME   EARL MILLER CO.
ADDRESS   22 RETTER ST., SAN DIEGO, CA 01211

Date	Explanation	Post Ref.	Debit	Credit	Cr. Balance

NAME   WOODY SMITH
ADDRESS   2 SPRING ST., WEERS, ND 02118

Date	Explanation	Post Ref.	Debit	Credit	Cr. Balance

PROBLEM A-5 (CONTINUED)

ACCOUNTS RECEIVABLE SUBSIDIARY LEDGER

NAME   BILL BURTON

ADDRESS   24 RYAN RD., BUIKE, OH 02183

Date	Explanation	Post Ref.	Debit	Credit	Dr. Balance

NAME   BONNIE FLOW CO.

ADDRESS   2 SMITH RD., DALLAS, TX 22210

Date	Explanation	Post Ref.	Debit	Credit	Dr. Balance

NAME   JIM REX

ADDRESS   1 SCHOOL ST., CLEVELAND, OH 22441

Date	Explanation	Post Ref.	Debit	Credit	Dr. Balance

PROBLEM A-5 (CONTINUED)

NAME   AMY ROSE
ADDRESS   18 VEEK RD., CHESTER, CT 80111

Date	Explanation	Post Ref.	Debit	Credit	Dr. Balance

GENERAL LEDGER

CASH   **ACCOUNT NO. 110**

Date	Explanation	Post Ref.	Debit	Credit	Balance Debit	Balance Credit

ACCOUNTS RECEIVABLE   **ACCOUNT NO. 112**

Date	Explanation	Post Ref.	Debit	Credit	Balance Debit	Balance Credit

PREPAID RENT   **ACCOUNT NO. 114**

Date	Explanation	Post Ref.	Debit	Credit	Balance Debit	Balance Credit

PROBLEM A-5 (CONTINUED)

DELIVERY TRUCK — ACCOUNT NO. 121

Date	Explanation	Post Ref.	Debit	Credit	Balance Debit	Balance Credit

ACCOUNTS PAYABLE — ACCOUNT NO. 210

Date	Explanation	Post Ref.	Debit	Credit	Balance Debit	Balance Credit

A. ELLEN, CAPITAL — ACCOUNT NO. 310

Date	Explanation	Post Ref.	Debit	Credit	Balance Debit	Balance Credit

TOY SALES — ACCOUNT NO. 410

Date	Explanation	Post Ref.	Debit	Credit	Balance Debit	Balance Credit

PROBLEM A-5 (CONTINUED)

SALES RETURNS AND ALLOWANCES — ACCOUNT NO. 412

Date	Explanation	Post Ref.	Debit	Credit	Balance Debit	Balance Credit

SALES DISCOUNTS — ACCOUNT NO. 414

Date	Explanation	Post Ref.	Debit	Credit	Balance Debit	Balance Credit

TOY PURCHASES — ACCOUNT NO. 510

Date	Explanation	Post Ref.	Debit	Credit	Balance Debit	Balance Credit

PURCHASES RETURNS AND ALLOWANCES — ACCOUNT NO. 512

Date	Explanation	Post Ref.	Debit	Credit	Balance Debit	Balance Credit

Name _____ Class _____ Date _____

PROBLEM A-5 (CONTINUED)

PURCHASES DISCOUNT   **ACCOUNT NO. 514**

Date	Explanation	Post Ref.	Debit	Credit	Balance Debit	Balance Credit

SALARIES EXPENSE   **ACCOUNT NO. 610**

Date	Explanation	Post Ref.	Debit	Credit	Balance Debit	Balance Credit

CLEANING EXPENSE   **ACCOUNT NO. 612**

Date	Explanation	Post Ref.	Debit	Credit	Balance Debit	Balance Credit

PROBLEM A-5 (CONCLUDED)

(4)

ABBY'S TOY HOUSE
SCHEDULE OF ACCOUNTS RECEIVABLE
MARCH 31, 200X

(4)

ABBY'S TOY HOUSE
SCHEDULE OF ACCOUNTS PAYABLE
MARCH 31, 200X

Preparing a Worksheet for a Merchandise Company

11

SELF-REVIEW QUIZ 11-1

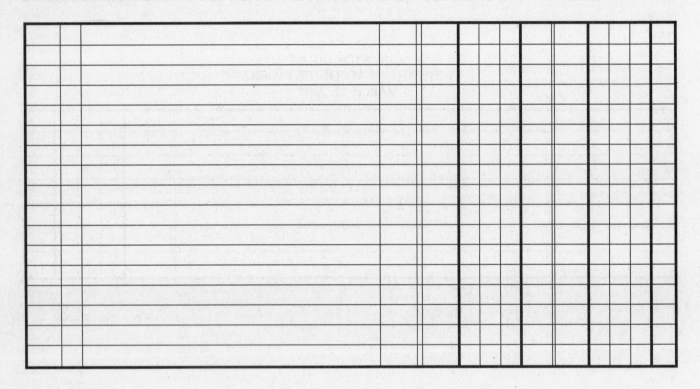

SELF-REVIEW QUIZ 11-2

Use one of the blank fold-out worksheets that accompanied your textbook.

Name _____ Class _____ Date _____

CHAPTER 11
FORMS FOR CLASSROOM DEMONSTRATION EXERCISES SET A OR SET B

1.

2.

3. A. _____   E. _____
    B. _____   F. _____
    C. _____
    D. _____

4. _____
   _____
   _____
   _____
   _____
   _____
   _____

5.
    A. _____ B. _____ C. _____ D. _____ E. _____ F. _____

Name _____ Class _____ Date _____

FORMS FOR EXERCISES

11-1.

A. _____
B. _____
C. _____
D. _____
E. _____
F. _____
G. _____
H. _____

11-2.

A. _____
_____

B. _____
_____

C. _____
_____

D. _____
_____

11-3.

Accounts Affected	Category	↑↓	Rules

11-4.

A. _____
B. _____
C. _____

11-5.

Use one of the blank fold-out worksheets that accompanied your textbook.

Name _____ Class _____ Date _____

END OF CHAPTER PROBLEMS

PROBLEM 11A-1 OR PROBLEM 11B-1

A.	
B.	
C.	
D.	

PROBLEM 11A-2 OR PROBLEM 11B-2;
PROBLEM 11A-3 OR PROBLEM 11B-3;
PROBLEM 11A-4 OR PROBLEM 11B-4

Use blank fold-out worksheets that accompanied your textbook.

Name _____ Class _____ Date _____

CHAPTER 11
SUMMARY PRACTICE TEST:
PREPARING A WORKSHEET
FOR A MERCHANDISE COMPANY

Part I Instructions

Fill in the blank(s) to complete the statement.

1. The _____ _____ system keeps a continual track of the quantity and cost of the inventory on hand.
2. In the periodic inventory system, new inventories bought is recorded in the _____ account.
3. A continuous record of inventory is kept in a(n) _____ _____ system.
4. When using the periodic system, _____ _____ will remain unchanged.
5. _____ _____ represents a liability on the balance sheet and records money received for a sale or service not yet performed.
6. Freight-in is _____ to the cost of goods sold.
7. Net Sales less Cost of Goods Sold equals _____ _____.
8. _____ _____ equals Gross Sales less Sales Discounts and Sales Returns and Allowances.
9. Net Purchases equals Purchases less _____ _____ and _____ _____ _____.
10. A(n) _____ _____ helps calculate ending inventory.
11. Ending inventory is _____ from the cost of goods available for sale.
12. Net purchases are _____ to Beginning Inventory to get the cost of goods available for sale.
13. Gross Profit less _____ equals Net Income.
14. Purchase discounts _____ the total cost of merchandise sold.
15. Beginning inventory at the end of the period is assumed to be _____, and thus a _____.
16. The ending inventory of one period becomes the _____ _____ next period.
17. Ending inventory represents goods not _____.
18. The inventory account is _____ at the end of the period.
19. Purchases are increased by a(n) _____.
20. Sales returns and allowances are used in calculating _____ _____.
21. Beginning Inventory plus Net Purchases equals _____ _____ _____ _____ _____.
22. Beginning Inventory and Ending Inventory are never _____ on the worksheet.

Name _____ Class _____ Date _____

Part II Instructions

Answer true or false to the following statements.
1. Unearned Revenue is a liability.
2. Perpetual inventory keeps a continuous record of inventory.
3. Purchases increase cost of goods sold.
4. Freight-in is added to cost of goods sold.
5. Figures for Beginning and Ending Inventory are combined on the worksheet.
6. A periodic system is used by companies with low volume and high unit prices.
7. Merchandise Inventory is an asset.
8. Unearned Revenue is a liability on the income statement.
9. Inventory is always taken 10 times per year.
10. Purchases replace ending inventory in a periodic system.
11. A trial balance may be placed directly on a worksheet.
12. The adjustment process updates the inventory account.
13. A post-closing trial balance has no temporary accounts.
14. Sales Discounts is a permanent account.
15. Gross sales are located on the balance sheet.
16. The Sales Returns and Allowances account has a normal balance of a credit.
17. Ending inventory of one period is the beginning inventory of the following period.
18. Net income always means cash.
19. Ending inventory increases cost of goods sold.
20. Net purchases is always the same as total purchases.
21. Gross profit plus expenses equals net income.
22. Unearned Storage Fees is a liability.
23. Merchandise inventory that is sold is assumed to be a cost.
24. Accumulated Depreciation is increased by a debit.
25. Merchandise Inventory can never be listed on a trial balance.
26. Ending Merchandise Inventory can only be found on a balance sheet.
27. The amount of rent expired is used in the adjustment process.
28. Adjustments help update individual ledger accounts.
29. Purchases Returns and Allowances is found on a balance sheet.
30. Beginning Merchandise Inventory found on the balance sheet from the prior period will also be placed in the cost of goods sold section of the balance sheet.
31. Sales always means cash received.
32. Ending Merchandise Inventory of the current period is found only on the balance sheet.
33. Purchases adds to the cost of goods sold.
34. Purchases discounts reduce the cost of purchases on the balance sheet.
35. Beginning inventory can never be assumed sold by the end of a period.

36. Ending inventory in one period becomes beginning inventory for the next two periods.
37. The ending inventory may be calculated from an inventory sheet.
38. Income Summary is used in the adjustment of merchandise inventory.
39. Ending inventory not sold is only placed in the credit column of the balance sheet section on the worksheet.
40. Purchases Discount is recorded in the credit column of the income statement section on the worksheet.
41. Gross profit and net income mean the same.
42. All companies must give sales discounts.
43. A merchandise company does not need a cost of goods sold section on the income statement.
44. Cost of goods available to sell less ending inventory equals cost of goods not sold.

SOLUTIONS TO SUMMARY PRACTICE TEST

Part I

1. perpetual inventory
2. Purchases
3. perpetual inventory
4. beginning inventory
5. Unearned Revenue
6. added
7. Gross Profit
8. Net sales
9. Purchases Discounts, Purchases Returns and Allowances
10. Inventory sheet (record)
11. subtracted
12. added
13. Expenses
14. reduce
15. sold, cost
16. begining inventory
17. sold
18. adjusted
19. debit
20. net sales
21. Cost of Goods Available for Sale
22. combined

Name _____ Class _____ Date _____

Part II

1. true	12. true	23. true	34. false
2. true	13. true	24. false	35. false
3. true	14. false	25. false	36. false
4. true	15. false	26. false	37. true
5. false	16. false	27. true	38. true
6. false	17. true	28. true	39. false
7. true	18. false	29. false	40. true
8. false	19. false	30. false	41. false
9. false	20. false	31. false	42. false
10. false	21. false	32. false	43. false
11. true	22. true	33. true	44. false

CONTINUING PROBLEM FOR CHAPTER 11

Use the blank fold-out worksheet that accompanied your textbook.

Completion of the Accounting Cycle for a Merchandise Company

12

SELF-REVIEW QUIZ 12-1

(1)

(2)

(3)

SELF-REVIEW QUIZ 12-2

GENERAL JOURNAL PAGE 2

Date	Account Titles and Description	PR	Dr.	Cr.

Name _____ Class _____ Date _____

SELF-REVIEW QUIZ 12-3

Situation 1
Situation 2
Situation 3

Name _____ Class _____ Date _____

CHAPTER 12
FORMS FOR CLASSROOM DEMONSTRATION EXERCISES SET A OR SET B

1. _____

2. _____

3. _____

4. A. _____   F. _____
    B. _____   G. _____
    C. _____   H. _____
    D. _____   I. _____
    E. _____   J. _____

5.

Name _____ Class _____ Date _____

FORMS FOR EXERCISES

12-1.

COST OF GOODS SOLD

Merchandise Inv. 12/01/X1 _____
Purchases _____
Less: Purchases Disc. _____
          Purch. R. & A. _____
           _____
Net Purchases _____
          Add: Freight-in _____
Net Cost of Purchases _____
Cost of Goods Available for Sale _____
Less: Merchandise Inv. 12/31/X1 _____
          Cost of Goods Sold _____

12-2.

A. _____
B. _____
C. _____
D. _____
E. _____
F. _____
G. _____

12-3.

EXERCISES (CONCLUDED)

12-4.

A. SLOW COMPANY
BALANCE SHEET
DECEMBER 31, 200X

12-5.

(A)

Salaries Expense Salaries Payable

(B)

Salaries Expense Salaries Expense

(C)

Salaries Expense Cash

END OF CHAPTER PROBLEMS

PROBLEM 12A-1 OR PROBLEM 12B-1

RING.COM
INCOME STATEMENT
FOR YEAR ENDED DECEMBER 31, 200X

PROBLEM 12A-2 OR PROBLEM 12B-2

JAMES CO.
STATEMENT OF OWNER'S EQUITY
FOR MONTH ENDED DECEMBER 31, 200X

PROBLEM 12A-2 OR PROBLEM 12B-2 (CONCLUDED)

JAMES CO.
BALANCE SHEET
DECEMBER 31, 200X

PROBLEM 12A-3 OR PROBLEM 12B-3

Use one of the blank fold-out worksheets that accompanied your textbook.

JAY'S SUPPLIES
INCOME STATEMENT
FOR YEAR ENDED DECEMBER 31, 200X

PROBLEM 12A-3 OR PROBLEM 12B-3 (CONTINUED)

JAY'S SUPPLIES
STATEMENT OF OWNER'S EQUITY
FOR YEAR ENDED DECEMBER 31, 200X

PROBLEM 12A-3 OR PROBLEM 12B-3 (CONTINUED)

JAY'S SUPPLIES
BALANCE SHEET
DECEMBER 31, 200X

Name _____ Class _____ Date _____

PROBLEM 12A-3 OR PROBLEM 12B-3 (CONTINUED)

GENERAL JOURNAL

PAGE 2

Date	Account Titles and Description	PR	Dr.	Cr.

SG-401

PROBLEM 12A-3 OR PROBLEM 12B-3 (CONCLUDED)
GENERAL JOURNAL

PAGE 3

Date	Account Titles and Description	PR	Dr.	Cr.

Name _____ Class _____ Date _____

PROBLEM 12A-4 OR PROBLEM 12B-4

Use one of the blank fold-out worksheets that accompanied your textbook.

CALLAHAN LUMBER
INCOME STATEMENT
FOR YEAR ENDED DECEMBER 31, 200X

SG-403

PROBLEM 12A-4 OR PROBLEM 12B-4 (CONTINUED)

Use one of the blank fold-out worksheets that accompanied your textbook.

CALLAHAN LUMBER
STATEMENT OF OWNER'S EQUITY
FOR YEAR ENDED DECEMBER 31, 200X

PROBLEM 12A-4 OR PROBLEM 12B-4 (CONTINUED)

CALLAHAN LUMBER
BALANCE SHEET
DECEMBER 31, 200X

PROBLEM 12A-4 OR PROBLEM 12B-4 (CONTINUED)

GENERAL JOURNAL

PAGE 2

Date	Account Titles and Description	PR	Dr.	Cr.

Name _____ Class _____ Date _____

PROBLEM 12A-4 OR PROBLEM 12B-4 (CONTINUED)

CALLAHAN LUMBER
GENERAL LEDGER

CASH   **ACCOUNT NO. 110**

Date	Explanation	Post Ref.	Debit	Credit	Balance Debit	Balance Credit

ACCOUNTS RECEIVABLE   **ACCOUNT NO. 111**

Date	Explanation	Post Ref.	Debit	Credit	Balance Debit	Balance Credit

MERCHANDISE INVENTORY   **ACCOUNT NO. 112**

Date	Explanation	Post Ref.	Debit	Credit	Balance Debit	Balance Credit

LUMBER SUPPLIES   **ACCOUNT NO. 113**

Date	Explanation	Post Ref.	Debit	Credit	Balance Debit	Balance Credit

PROBLEM 12A-4 OR PROBLEM 12B-4 (CONTINUED)

PREPAID INSURANCE — ACCOUNT NO. **114**

Date	Explanation	Post Ref.	Debit	Credit	Balance Debit	Balance Credit

LUMBER EQUIPMENT — ACCOUNT NO. **121**

Date	Explanation	Post Ref.	Debit	Credit	Balance Debit	Balance Credit

ACCUMULATED DEPRECIATION, LUMBER EQUIPMENT — ACCOUNT NO. **122**

Date	Explanation	Post Ref.	Debit	Credit	Balance Debit	Balance Credit

ACCOUNTS PAYABLE — ACCOUNT NO. **220**

Date	Explanation	Post Ref.	Debit	Credit	Balance Debit	Balance Credit

WAGES PAYABLE — ACCOUNT NO. **221**

Date	Explanation	Post Ref.	Debit	Credit	Balance Debit	Balance Credit

PROBLEM 12A-4 OR PROBLEM 12B-4 (CONTINUED)

J. CALLAHAN, CAPITAL   ACCOUNT NO. 330

Date	Explanation	Post Ref.	Debit	Credit	Balance Debit	Balance Credit

J. CALLAHAN, WITHDRAWALS   ACCOUNT NO. 331

Date	Explanation	Post Ref.	Debit	Credit	Balance Debit	Balance Credit

INCOME SUMMARY   ACCOUNT NO. 332

Date	Explanation	Post Ref.	Debit	Credit	Balance Debit	Balance Credit

SALES   ACCOUNT NO. 440

Date	Explanation	Post Ref.	Debit	Credit	Balance Debit	Balance Credit

SALES RETURNS AND ALLOWANCES   ACCOUNT NO. 441

Date	Explanation	Post Ref.	Debit	Credit	Balance Debit	Balance Credit

PROBLEM 12A-4 OR PROBLEM 12B-4 (CONTINUED)

PURCHASES — ACCOUNT NO. **550**

Date	Explanation	Post Ref.	Debit	Credit	Balance Debit	Balance Credit

PURCHASES DISCOUNT — ACCOUNT NO. **551**

Date	Explanation	Post Ref.	Debit	Credit	Balance Debit	Balance Credit

PURCHASES RETURNS AND ALLOWANCES — ACCOUNT NO. **552**

Date	Explanation	Post Ref.	Debit	Credit	Balance Debit	Balance Credit

WAGES EXPENSE — ACCOUNT NO. **660**

Date	Explanation	Post Ref.	Debit	Credit	Balance Debit	Balance Credit

ADVERTISING EXPENSE — ACCOUNT NO. **661**

Date	Explanation	Post Ref.	Debit	Credit	Balance Debit	Balance Credit

Name _____ Class _____ Date _____

PROBLEM 12A-4 OR PROBLEM 12B-4 (CONTINUED)

RENT EXPENSE — ACCOUNT NO. 662

Date	Explanation	Post Ref.	Debit	Credit	Balance Debit	Balance Credit

DEPRECIATION EXPENSE, LUMBER EQUIPMENT — ACCOUNT NO. 663

Date	Explanation	Post Ref.	Debit	Credit	Balance Debit	Balance Credit

LUMBER SUPPLIES EXPENSE — ACCOUNT NO. 664

Date	Explanation	Post Ref.	Debit	Credit	Balance Debit	Balance Credit

INSURANCE EXPENSE — ACCOUNT NO. 665

Date	Explanation	Post Ref.	Debit	Credit	Balance Debit	Balance Credit

PROBLEM 12A-4 OR PROBLEM 12B-4 (CONCLUDED)

CALLAHAN LUMBER
POST-CLOSING TRIAL BALANCE
DECEMBER 31, 200X

	Dr.	Cr.

Name _____ Class _____ Date _____

CHAPTER 12
SUMMARY PRACTICE TEST:
COMPLETION OF THE ACCOUNTING
CYCLE FOR A MERCHANDISE COMPANY

Part I Instructions

Fill in the blank(s) to complete the statement.

1. There are no debits or credits on _____ _____.

2. The formal income statement uses _____ _____ figures for inventory.

3. The gross profit figure _____ (is/is not) found on the worksheet.

4. _____ expenses are related to the general activity.

5. _____ _____ are related to the administrative function.

6. _____ _____ could be broken down into selling and administrative expenses.

7. The _____ figure for capital is not found on the worksheet.

8. _____ _____ are cash or other assets that will be converted into cash during the normal operating cycle of the company or one year, whichever is longer.

9. _____ and _____ are long-lived assets used for the production or sale of other assets or services.

10. Debts or obligations that are to be paid with current assets within one year or one operating cycle are called _____ _____.

11. Mortgage Payable is an example of a(n) _____ _____ _____.

12. Ending merchandise inventory is a(n) _____ _____.

13. By the adjusting process, the beginning inventory of the period is transferred to _____ _____.

14. The _____ _____ _____ _____ contains no temporary accounts.

15. A reversing entry involves certain _____ entries.

16. Reversing entries are used only if assets are _____ and have no previous balance and liabilities are _____ and have no balance.

SG-413

Name _____ Class _____ Date _____

Part II Instructions

Match the term in the last column to the definition, example, or phrase in the right column. Be sure to use a letter only once.

____d____ 1. EXAMPLE: Computer Equipment
_____ 2. Net Sales-Cost of Goods Sold
_____ 3. Operating Cycle
_____ 4. Inside Columns of Financial Reports
_____ 5. Gross Profit-Operating Expenses
_____ 6. Operating Expenses
_____ 7. Temporary Account
_____ 8. OASDI
_____ 9. Result of an adjusting entry
_____ 10. Petty Cash
_____ 11. An asset that is adjsuted
_____ 12. Ending Capital
_____ 13. A Liability showing revenue no earned
_____ 14. Unearned training fees

a. Subtotaling
b. Unearned Revenue
c. Current asset
d. Plant and Equipment
e. Reversing Entry
f. Time Period
g. Net Income
h. Current Liability
i. When earned reduced by a debit
j. Gross Profit
k. Merchandise Inventory
l. Debit Balance
m. Not found on worksheet
n. Income Summary
o. Selling and Administrative

Part III Instructions

Answer true or false to the following statements.

1. A balance sheet records all revenue.
2. Cost of goods sold contains only ending inventory.
3. Net sales less cost of goods sold equals gross profit.
4. Operating expenses can only be administrative.
5. Supplies is part of Plant and Equipment.
6. Unearned Rent is an asset.
7. An operating cycle of a business must be one year.
8. Accumulated Depreciation is a current asset.
9. Long-term liabilities are due within one year.
10. Merchandise Inventory is a temporary account.
11. The normal balance of merchandise inventory is a debit.
12. The post-closing trial balance will not contain any unearned revenue accounts.
13. Ending inventory is closed directly to Capital.
14. Reversing entries cannot be applied to all adjustments.
15. Reversing entries are optional at the end of each month before the close of the year.
16. Reversing entries switch closing entries on the first day of the new period.
17. An adjusting entry with an asset decreasing with no prevoius balance cannot be reversed.
18. Closing entries will update the merchandise inventory account.
19. Beginning merchandise inventory of a period is assumed sold by the end of the period.
20. An adjusting entry for Accrued Wages can be reversed.

CHAPTER 12
SOLUTIONS TO SUMMARY PRACTICE TEST

Part I

1. financial reports
2. two separate
3. is not
4. General
5. Administrative expenses
6. Operating expenses
7. ending
8. Current assets
9. Plant, Equipment
10. current liabilities
11. long-term liability
12. permanent account
13. Income Summary
14. post-closing trial balance
15. adjusting
16. increasing, increasing

Part II

1. d
2. j
3. f
4. a
5. g
6. o
7. n
8. h
9. e
10. l
11. k
12. m
13. b
14. i

Part III

1. false
2. false
3. true
4. false
5. false
6. false
7. false
8. false
9. false
10. false
11. true
12. false
13. false
14. true
15. false
16. false
17. true
18. false
19. true
20. true

CONTINUING PROBLEM FOR CHAPTER 12

SANCHEZ COMPUTER CENTER
GENERAL JOURNAL

PAGE 12

Date	Account Titles and Description	PR	Dr.	Cr.

SANCHEZ COMPUTER CENTER
GENERAL LEDGER

CASH
ACCOUNT NO. 1000

Date		Explanation	Post Ref.	Debit	Credit	Balance Debit	Balance Credit
3/1	0X	Balance forward	✔			12 5 16 65	

PETTY CASH
ACCOUNT NO. 1010

Date		Explanation	Post Ref.	Debit	Credit	Balance Debit	Balance Credit
3/1	0X	Balance forward	✔			1 0 0 00	

ACCOUNTS RECEIVABLE
ACCOUNT NO. 1020

Date		Explanation	Post Ref.	Debit	Credit	Balance Debit	Balance Credit
3/1	0X	Balance forward	✔			11 9 0 0 00	

PREPAID RENT
ACCOUNT NO. 1025

Date		Explanation	Post Ref.	Debit	Credit	Balance Debit	Balance Credit
3/1	0X	Balance forward	✔			2 8 0 0 00	

SUPPLIES
ACCOUNT NO. 1030

Date		Explanation	Post Ref.	Debit	Credit	Balance Debit	Balance Credit
3/1	0X	Balance forward	✔			432 00	

MERCHANDISE INVENTORY
ACCOUNT NO. 1040

Date		Explanation	Post Ref.	Debit	Credit	Balance Debit	Balance Credit

COMPUTER SHOP EQUIPMENT
ACCOUNT NO. 1080

Date		Explanation	Post Ref.	Debit	Credit	Balance Debit	Balance Credit
3/1	0X	Balance forward	✔			3 800 00	

ACCUMULATED DEPRECIATION, C.S. EQUIPMENT
ACCOUNT NO. 1081

Date		Explanation	Post Ref.	Debit	Credit	Balance Debit	Balance Credit
3/1	0X	Balance forward	✔				99 00

OFFICE EQUIPMENT
ACCOUNT NO. 1090

Date		Explanation	Post Ref.	Debit	Credit	Balance Debit	Balance Credit
3/1	0X	Balance forward	✔			1 050 00	

ACCUMULATED DEPRECIATION, OFFICE EQUIPMENT ACCOUNT NO. **1091**

Date		Explanation	Post Ref.	Debit	Credit	Balance Debit	Balance Credit
3/1	0X	Balance forward	✔				2 0 00

ACCOUNTS PAYABLE ACCOUNT NO. **2000**

Date		Explanation	Post Ref.	Debit	Credit	Balance Debit	Balance Credit
3/1	0X	Balance forward	✔				2 8 4 0 00

WAGES PAYABLE ACCOUNT NO. **2010**

Date		Explanation	Post Ref.	Debit	Credit	Balance Debit	Balance Credit

FICA OASDI PAYABLE ACCOUNT NO. **2020**

Date		Explanation	Post Ref.	Debit	Credit	Balance Debit	Balance Credit

FICA MEDICARE PAYABLE ACCOUNT NO. **2030**

Date		Explanation	Post Ref.	Debit	Credit	Balance Debit	Balance Credit

FIT PAYABLE — ACCOUNT NO. **2040**

Date	Explanation	Post Ref.	Debit	Credit	Balance Debit	Balance Credit

SIT PAYABLE — ACCOUNT NO. **2050**

Date	Explanation	Post Ref.	Debit	Credit	Balance Debit	Balance Credit

FUTA PAYABLE — ACCOUNT NO. **2060**

Date	Explanation	Post Ref.	Debit	Credit	Balance Debit	Balance Credit

SUTA PAYABLE — ACCOUNT NO. **2070**

Date	Explanation	Post Ref.	Debit	Credit	Balance Debit	Balance Credit

T. FREEDMAN, CAPITAL — ACCOUNT NO. **3000**

Date	Explanation	Post Ref.	Debit	Credit	Balance Debit	Balance Credit
3/1 0X	Balance forward	✓				7 4 0 6 00

T. FREEDMAN WITHDRAWALS — ACCOUNT NO. 3010

Date		Explanation	Post Ref.	Debit	Credit	Balance Debit	Balance Credit
3/1	0X	Balance forward	✓			2 015 00	

INCOME SUMMARY — ACCOUNT NO. 3020

Date	Explanation	Post Ref.	Debit	Credit	Balance Debit	Balance Credit

SERVICE REVENUE — ACCOUNT NO. 4000

Date		Explanation	Post Ref.	Debit	Credit	Balance Debit	Balance Credit
3/1	0X	Balance forward	✓				19 800 00

SALES — ACCOUNT NO. 4010

Date		Explanation	Post Ref.	Debit	Credit	Balance Debit	Balance Credit
3/1	0X	Balance forward	✓				9 700 00

GENERAL LEDGER

SALES RETURNS AND ALLOWANCES   **ACCOUNT NO. 4020**

Date		Explanation	Post Ref.	Debit	Credit	Balance Debit	Balance Credit
3/1	0X	Balance forward	✔			400 00	

SALES DISCOUNTS   **ACCOUNT NO. 4030**

Date		Explanation	Post Ref.	Debit	Credit	Balance Debit	Balance Credit
3/1	0X	Balance forward	✔			220 00	

ADVERTISING EXPENSE   **ACCOUNT NO. 5010**

Date		Explanation	Post Ref.	Debit	Credit	Balance Debit	Balance Credit
3/1	0X	Balance forward	✔			800 00	

RENT EXPENSE   **ACCOUNT NO. 5020**

Date		Explanation	Post Ref.	Debit	Credit	Balance Debit	Balance Credit

UTILITIES EXPENSE   **ACCOUNT NO. 5030**

Date		Explanation	Post Ref.	Debit	Credit	Balance Debit	Balance Credit
3/1	0X	Balance forward	✔			290 00	

PHONE EXPENSE ACCOUNT NO. 5040

Date		Explanation	Post Ref.	Debit	Credit	Balance Debit	Balance Credit
3/1	0X	Balance forward	✔			150 00	

SUPPLIES EXPENSE ACCOUNT NO. 5050

Date		Explanation	Post Ref.	Debit	Credit	Balance Debit	Balance Credit

INSURANCE EXPENSE ACCOUNT NO. 5060

Date		Explanation	Post Ref.	Debit	Credit	Balance Debit	Balance Credit
3/1	0X	Balance forward	✔			100 00	

POSTAGE EXPENSE ACCOUNT NO. 5070

Date		Explanation	Post Ref.	Debit	Credit	Balance Debit	Balance Credit
3/1	0X	Balance forward	✔			175 00	

DEPRECIATION EXPENSE C.S. EQUIPMENT ACCOUNT NO. 5080

Date		Explanation	Post Ref.	Debit	Credit	Balance Debit	Balance Credit

Name _____ Class _____ Date _____

DEPRECIATION EXPENSE OFFICE EQUIPMENT   ACCOUNT NO. 5090

Date	Explanation	Post Ref.	Debit	Credit	Balance Debit	Balance Credit

MISCELLANEOUS EXPENSE   ACCOUNT NO. 5100

Date	Explanation	Post Ref.	Debit	Credit	Balance Debit	Balance Credit
3/1 0X	Balance forward	✓			1 0 00	

WAGE EXPENSE   ACCOUNT NO. 5110

Date	Explanation	Post Ref.	Debit	Credit	Balance Debit	Balance Credit
3/1 0X	Balance forward	✓			2 0 3 0 00	

PAYROLL TAX EXPENSE   ACCOUNT NO. 5120

Date	Explanation	Post Ref.	Debit	Credit	Balance Debit	Balance Credit
3/1 0X	Balance forward	✓			2 2 6 35	

INTEREST EXPENSE   ACCOUNT NO. 5130

Date	Explanation	Post Ref.	Debit	Credit	Balance Debit	Balance Credit

BAD DEBT EXPENSE — ACCOUNT NO. 5140

Date	Explanation	Post Ref.	Debit	Credit	Balance Debit	Balance Credit

PURCHASES — ACCOUNT NO. 6000

Date	Explanation	Post Ref.	Debit	Credit	Balance Debit	Balance Credit
3/1 0X	Balance forward	✓			950 00	

PURCHASE RETURNS AND ALLOWANCES — ACCOUNT NO. 6010

Date	Explanation	Post Ref.	Debit	Credit	Balance Debit	Balance Credit
3/1 0X	Balance forward	✓				100 00

PURCHASE DISCOUNTS — ACCOUNT NO. 6020

Date	Explanation	Post Ref.	Debit	Credit	Balance Debit	Balance Credit

FREIGHT IN — ACCOUNT NO. 6030

Date	Explanation	Post Ref.	Debit	Credit	Balance Debit	Balance Credit

SANCHEZ COMPUTER CENTER
INCOME STATEMENT
FOR THE SIX MONTHS ENDED MARCH 31, 200X

SANCHEZ COMPUTER CENTER
STATEMENT OF OWNER'S EQUITY
FOR THE SIX MONTHS ENDED MARCH 31, 200X

Name _____ Class _____ Date _____

SANCHEZ COMPUTER CENTER
BALANCE SHEET
MARCH 31, 200X

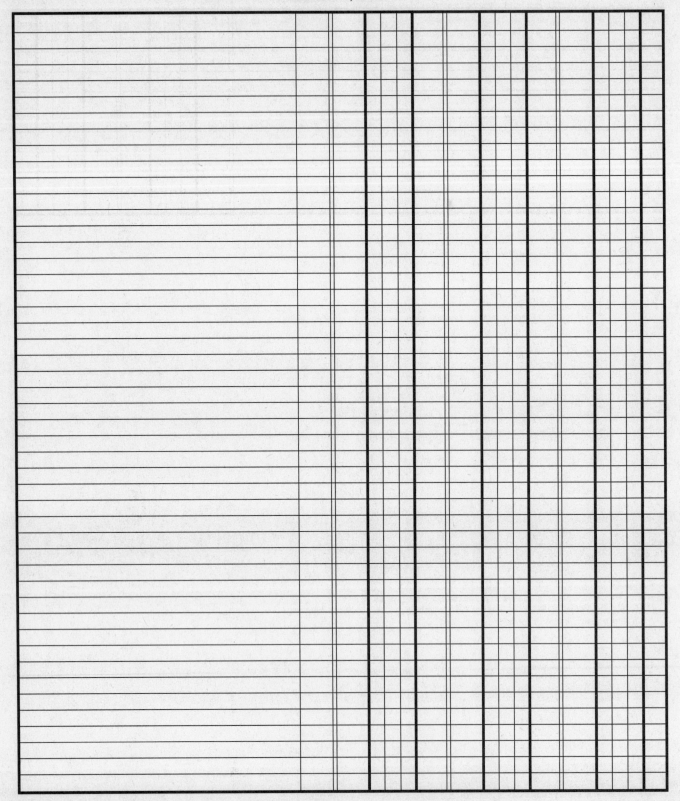

SG-428

Name _____ Class _____ Date _____

MINI PRACTICE SET

THE CORNER DRESS SHOP
GENERAL JOURNAL

PAGE 4

Date	Account Titles and Description	PR	Dr.	Cr.

THE CORNER DRESS SHOP

Use a blank fold-out worksheet and a blank payroll register that accompanied your textbook.

Name _____ Class _____ Date _____

MINI PRACTICE SET
Use the blank fold-out worksheets that accompanied your textbook.

THE CORNER DRESS SHOP
GENERAL JOURNAL PAGE 5

Date	Account Titles and Description	PR	Dr.	Cr.

Name _____ Class _____ Date _____

MINI PRACTICE SET

THE CORNER DRESS SHOP
GENERAL JOURNAL

PAGE 6

Date	Account Titles and Description	PR	Dr.	Cr.

SG-431

MINI PRACTICE SET

THE CORNER DRESS SHOP
GENERAL JOURNAL

PAGE 7

Date	Account Titles and Description	PR	Dr.	Cr.

MINI PRACTICE SET

THE CORNER DRESS SHOP
GENERAL JOURNAL

PAGE 8

Date	Account Titles and Description	PR	Dr.	Cr.

MINI PRACTICE SET

THE CORNER DRESS SHOP
GENERAL JOURNAL

PAGE 9

Date	Account Titles and Description	PR	Dr.	Cr.

MINI PRACTICE SET

THE CORNER DRESS SHOP
AUXILIARY PETTY CASH RECORD

Date	Voucher No.	Description	Receipts	Payment	Category of Payment				
					Postage Expense	Delivery Expense	Sundry	
							Account	Amount

Name _____ Class _____ Date _____

MINI PRACTICE SET

ACCOUNTS PAYABLE SUBSIDIARY LEDGER

NAME BLEW CO.

Date 200X		Explanation	Post Ref.	Debit	Credit	Credit Balance
Mar	1	Balance	✔			1 9 0 0 00

NAME JONES CO.

Date 200X		Explanation	Post Ref.	Debit	Credit	Credit Balance

NAME MOE'S GARAGE

Date 200X		Explanation	Post Ref.	Debit	Credit	Credit Balance

MINI PRACTICE SET

NAME   MORRIS CO.

Date 200X	Explanation	Post Ref.	Debit	Credit	Credit Balance

ACCOUNTS RECEIVABLE SUBSIDIARY LEDGER

NAME   BING CO.

Date 200X		Explanation	Post Ref.	Debit	Credit	Debit Balance
Mar	1	Balance	✓			2 2 0 0 00

NAME   BLEW CO.

Date 200X	Explanation	Post Ref.	Debit	Credit	Debit Balance

MINI PRACTICE SET
NAME RONALD CO.

Date 200X	Explanation	Post Ref.	Debit	Credit	Debit Balance

GENERAL LEDGER

CASH   **ACCOUNT NO. 110**

Date 200X	Explanation	Post Ref.	Debit	Credit	Balance Debit	Balance Credit
Mar 1	Balance	✔			2,231 90	

SG-438

Name _____ Class _____ Date _____

MINI PRACTICE SET

ACCOUNTS RECEIVABLE   **ACCOUNT NO. 111**

Date 200X		Explanation	Post Ref.	Debit	Credit	Balance Debit	Balance Credit
Mar	1	Balance	✓			2 200 00	

PETTY CASH   **ACCOUNT NO. 112**

Date 200X		Explanation	Post Ref.	Debit	Credit	Balance Debit	Balance Credit
Mar	1	Balance	✓			35 00	

MERCHANDISE INVENTORY   **ACCOUNT NO. 114**

Date 200X		Explanation	Post Ref.	Debit	Credit	Balance Debit	Balance Credit
Mar	1	Balance	✓			5 600 00	

MINI PRACTICE SET

PREPAID RENT ACCOUNT NO. 116

Date 200X		Explanation	Post Ref.	Debit	Credit	Balance Debit	Balance Credit
Mar	1	Balance	✓			1 8 0 0 00	

DELIVERY TRUCK ACCOUNT NO. 120

Date 200X		Explanation	Post Ref.	Debit	Credit	Balance Debit	Balance Credit
Mar	1	Balance	✓			6 0 0 0 00	

ACCUMULATED DEPRECIATION, TRUCK ACCOUNT NO. 121

Date 200X		Explanation	Post Ref.	Debit	Credit	Balance Debit	Balance Credit
Mar	1	Balance	✓				1 5 0 0 00

MINI PRACTICE SET

ACCOUNTS PAYABLE   ACCOUNT NO. 210

Date 200X		Explanation	Post Ref.	Debit	Credit	Balance Debit	Balance Credit
Mar	1	Balance	✓				1 900 00

SALARIES PAYABLE   ACCOUNT NO. 212

Date 200X		Explanation	Post Ref.	Debit	Credit	Balance Debit	Balance Credit

FIT PAYABLE   ACCOUNT NO. 214

Date 200X		Explanation	Post Ref.	Debit	Credit	Balance Debit	Balance Credit
Mar	1	Balance	✓				1 013 00

Name _____ Class _____ Date _____

MINI PRACTICE SET

FICA-OASDI PAYABLE — ACCOUNT NO. 216

Date 200X	Explanation	Post Ref.	Debit	Credit	Balance Debit	Balance Credit
Mar 1	Balance	✔				1 339 20

FICA-MEDICARE PAYABLE — ACCOUNT NO. 218

Date 200X	Explanation	Post Ref.	Debit	Credit	Balance Debit	Balance Credit
Mar 1	Balance	✔				313 20

SIT PAYABLE — ACCOUNT NO. 220

Date 200X	Explanation	Post Ref.	Debit	Credit	Balance Debit	Balance Credit
Mar 1	Balance	✔				756 00

SUTA TAX PAYABLE — ACCOUNT NO. 222

Date 200X	Explanation	Post Ref.	Debit	Credit	Balance Debit	Balance Credit
Mar 1	Balance	✔				979 20

FUTA TAX PAYABLE — ACCOUNT NO. 224

Date 200X	Explanation	Post Ref.	Debit	Credit	Balance Debit	Balance Credit
Mar 1	Balance	✔				163 20

UNEARNED RENT — ACCOUNT NO. 226

Date 200X	Explanation	Post Ref.	Debit	Credit	Balance Debit	Balance Credit
Mar 1	Balance	✔				800 00

MINI PRACTICE SET

B. LOEB, CAPITAL   ACCOUNT NO. 310

Date 200X	Explanation	Post Ref.	Debit	Credit	Balance Debit	Balance Credit
Mar 1	Balance	✓				9 1 0 3 10

B. LOEB, WITHDRAWALS   ACCOUNT NO. 320

Date 200X	Explanation	Post Ref.	Debit	Credit	Balance Debit	Balance Credit

INCOME SUMMARY   ACCOUNT NO. 330

Date 200X	Explanation	Post Ref.	Debit	Credit	Balance Debit	Balance Credit

SALES   ACCOUNT NO. 410

Date 200X	Explanation	Post Ref.	Debit	Credit	Balance Debit	Balance Credit

SALES RETURNS AND ALLOWANCES   ACCOUNT NO. 412

Date 200X	Explanation	Post Ref.	Debit	Credit	Balance Debit	Balance Credit

Name _____ Class _____ Date _____

MINI PRACTICE SET

SALES DISCOUINT   **ACCOUNT NO. 414**

Date 200X	Explanation	Post Ref.	Debit	Credit	Balance Debit	Balance Credit

RENTAL INCOME   **ACCOUNT NO. 416**

Date 200X	Explanation	Post Ref.	Debit	Credit	Balance Debit	Balance Credit

PURCHASES   **ACCOUNT NO. 510**

Date 200X	Explanation	Post Ref.	Debit	Credit	Balance Debit	Balance Credit

PURCHASES RETURNS AND ALLOWANCES   **ACCOUNT NO. 512**

Date 200X	Explanation	Post Ref.	Debit	Credit	Balance Debit	Balance Credit

PURCHASES DISCOUNT   **ACCOUNT NO. 514**

Date 200X	Explanation	Post Ref.	Debit	Credit	Balance Debit	Balance Credit

MINI PRACTICE SET

SALES SALARY EXPENSE   **ACCOUNT NO. 610**

Date 200X	Explanation	Post Ref.	Debit	Credit	Balance Debit	Balance Credit

OFFICE SALARY EXPENSE   **ACCOUNT NO. 611**

Date 200X	Explanation	Post Ref.	Debit	Credit	Balance Debit	Balance Credit

PAYROLL TAX EXPENSE   **ACCOUNT NO. 612**

Date 200X	Explanation	Post Ref.	Debit	Credit	Balance Debit	Balance Credit

CLEANING EXPENSE   **ACCOUNT NO. 614**

Date 200X	Explanation	Post Ref.	Debit	Credit	Balance Debit	Balance Credit

DEPRECIATION EXPENSE, TRUCK   **ACCOUNT NO. 616**

Date 200X	Explanation	Post Ref.	Debit	Credit	Balance Debit	Balance Credit

Name _____ Class _____ Date _____

MINI PRACTICE SET

RENT EXPENSE ACCOUNT NO. **618**

Date 200X	Explanation	Post Ref.	Debit	Credit	Balance Debit	Balance Credit

POSTAGE EXPENSE ACCOUNT NO. **620**

Date 200X	Explanation	Post Ref.	Debit	Credit	Balance Debit	Balance Credit

DELIVERY EXPENSE ACCOUNT NO. **622**

Date 200X	Explanation	Post Ref.	Debit	Credit	Balance Debit	Balance Credit

MISCELLANEOUS EXPENSE ACCOUNT NO. **624**

Date 200X	Explanation	Post Ref.	Debit	Credit	Balance Debit	Balance Credit

Name _____ Class _____ Date _____

MINI PRACTICE SET

THE CORNER DRESS SHOP
SCHEDULE OF ACCOUNTS RECEIVABLE
MARCH 31, 200X

THE CORNER DRESS SHOP
SCHEDULE OF ACCOUNTS PAYABLE
MARCH 31, 200X

MINI PRACTICE SET

THE CORNER DRESS SHOP
INCOME STATEMENT
FOR MONTH ENDED MARCH 31, 200X

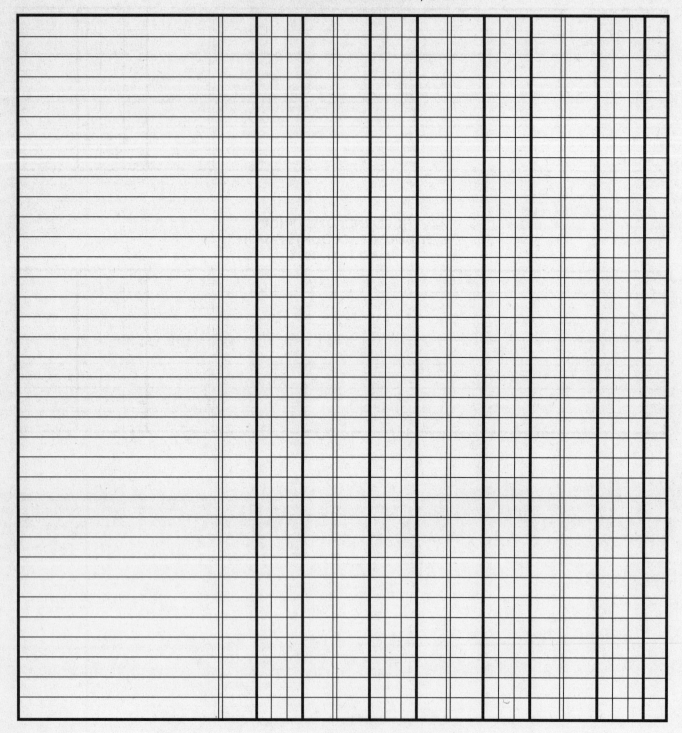

MINI PRACTICE SET

THE CORNER DRESS SHOP
STATEMENT OF OWNER'S EQUITY
FOR MONTH ENDED MARCH 31, 200X

MINI PRACTICE SET

THE CORNER DRESS SHOP
BALANCE SHEET
MARCH 31, 200X

Name _____ Class _____ Date _____

MINI PRACTICE SET

THE CORNER DRESS SHOP
POST-CLOSING TRIAL BALANCE
MARCH 31, 200X

Name _____ Class _____ Date _____

MINI PRACTICE SET

Form **941 for 200X:** Employer's QUARTERLY Federal Tax Return
(Rev. January 2006)
Department of the Treasury — Internal Revenue Service

990106
OMB No. 1545-0029

(EIN) Employer identification number ☐☐ – ☐☐☐☐☐☐☐

Name *(not your trade name)* _____

Trade name *(if any)* _____

Address
Number   Street   Suite or room number
City   State   ZIP code

Report for this Quarter ...
(Check one.)
☐ 1: January, February, March
☐ 2: April, May, June
☐ 3: July, August, September
☐ 4: October, November, December

Read the separate instructions before you fill out this form. Please type or print within the boxes.

Part 1: Answer these questions for this quarter.

1. Number of employees who received wages, tips, or other compensation for the pay period including: *Mar. 12* (Quarter 1), *June 12* (Quarter 2), *Sept. 12* (Quarter 3), *Dec. 12* (Quarter 4) **1** ☐

2. Wages, tips, and other compensation . . . . **2** ☐

3. Total income tax withheld from wages, tips, and other compensation . . . . **3** ☐

4. If no wages, tips, and other compensation are subject to social security or Medicare tax . . ☐ Check and go to line 6.

5. Taxable social security and Medicare wages and tips:

	Column 1		Column 2
5a Taxable social security wages	☐	× .124 =	☐
5b Taxable social security tips	☐	× .124 =	☐
5c Taxable Medicare wages & tips	☐	× .029 =	☐

   5d Total social security and Medicare taxes (*Column 2*, lines 5a + 5b + 5c = line 5d) . . **5d** ☐

6. Total taxes before adjustments (lines 3 + 5d = line 6) . . . . **6** ☐

7. **TAX ADJUSTMENTS** (Read the instructions for line 7 before completing lines 7a through 7h.):

   7a Current quarter's fractions of cents . . . . ☐

   7b Current quarter's sick pay . . . . ☐

   7c Current quarter's adjustments for tips and group-term life insurance ☐

   7d Current year's income tax withholding (attach Form 941c) . . ☐

   7e Prior quarters' social security and Medicare taxes (attach Form 941c) ☐

   7f Special additions to federal income tax (attach Form 941c) . . ☐

   7g Special additions to social security and Medicare (attach Form 941c) ☐

   7h **TOTAL ADJUSTMENTS** (Combine all amounts: lines 7a through 7g.) . . . . **7h** ☐

8. Total taxes after adjustments (Combine lines 6 and 7h.) . . . . **8** ☐

9. Advance earned income credit (EIC) payments made to employees . . . . **9** ☐

10. Total taxes after adjustment for advance EIC (line 8 – line 9 = line 10) . . . . . **10** ☐

11. Total deposits for this quarter, including overpayment applied from a prior quarter . . **11** ☐

12. Balance due (If line 10 is more than line 11, write the difference here.) . . . . . . **12** ☐
    Make checks payable to *United States Treasury*.

13. Overpayment (If line 11 is more than line 10, write the difference here.) ☐   Check one ☐ Apply to next return.
                                                                                        ☐ Send a refund.

▶ You **MUST** fill out both pages of this form and **SIGN** it.

Next ➡

For Privacy Act and Paperwork Reduction Act Notice, see the back of the Payment Voucher.   Cat. No. 17001Z   Form **941** (Rev. 1-2006)

SG-452

Name _____ Class _____ Date _____

MINI PRACTICE SET

990206

Name *(not your trade name)* | **Employer identification number (EIN)**

Part 2: Tell us about your deposit schedule and tax liability for this quarter.

If you are unsure about whether you are a monthly schedule depositor or a semiweekly schedule depositor, see *Pub. 15 (Circular E)*, section 11.

14 ☐☐ Write the state abbreviation for the state where you made your deposits OR write "MU" if you made your deposits in *multiple* states.

15 Check one: ☐ Line 10 is less than $2,500. Go to Part 3.

☐ You were a monthly schedule depositor for the entire quarter. Fill out your tax liability for each month. Then go to Part 3.

Tax liability: Month 1 _____
Month 2 _____
Month 3 _____

Total liability for quarter _____ Total must equal line 10.

☐ You were a semiweekly schedule depositor for any part of this quarter. Fill out *Schedule B (Form 941): Report of Tax Liability for Semiweekly Schedule Depositors,* and attach it to this form.

Part 3: Tell us about your business. If a question does NOT apply to your business, leave it blank.

16 If your business has closed or you stopped paying wages . . . . ☐ Check here, and

enter the final date you paid wages ___/___/___ .

17 If you are a seasonal employer and you do not have to file a return for every quarter of the year . . ☐ Check here.

Part 4: May we speak with your third-party designee?

Do you want to allow an employee, a paid tax preparer, or another person to discuss this return with the IRS? See the instructions for details.

☐ Yes. Designee's name _____

Phone (___) ___ - ____   Personal Identification Number (PIN) ☐☐☐☐☐

☐ No.

Part 5: Sign here. You MUST fill out both sides of this form and SIGN it.

Under penalties of perjury, I declare that I have examined this return, including accompanying schedules and statements, and to the best of my knowledge and belief, it is true, correct, and complete.

✗ Sign your name here _____

Print name and title _____

Date ___/___/___   Phone (___) ___ - ____

Part 6: For PAID preparers only *(optional)*

Paid Preparer's Signature _____

Firm's name _____

Address _____   EIN _____

_____   ZIP code _____

Date ___/___/___   Phone (___) ___ - ____   SSN/PTIN _____

☐ Check if you are self-employed.

Page **2**   Form **941** (Rev. 1-2006)

SG-453